WORKING WITH CHILDREN WITH
LEARNING AND BEHAVIOUR DISORDERS

YES THEY CAN

CLARA M. RICKETTS

FOREWORD BY REV. DR. DEVON DICK

Extra MILE Innovators
Kingston, Jamaica WI

.   .   .   .   .

Published by
Extra MILE Innovators
54 Montgomery Avenue,
Kingston 10, Jamaica W.I.
www.extramileja.com
ruthtaylor@extramileja.com
Tele: (1876) 782-9893

Cover, Layout and eBook by
N.D. Author Services [NDAS]
www.NDAuthorServices.com

AUTHOR CONTACT
cmaudrick@hotmail.com
surefoundation05@gmail.com
876-924-4495

DEDICATION

I dedicate this book to my son,
Richard,
who inspired me to write it,
and to the students of
Sure Foundation Educational Centre,
past, present, and future.

Richard

ENDORSEMENTS

Yes They Can! brings to life the experiences of children with "invisible disabilities,"—in particular students with behavior challenges—through the various case studies. The book also provides a detailed description of the model used at Sure Foundation, so that other institutions can replicate this excellent, results-driven programme. A great resource for professionals in the field which is applicable to the Jamaican context.

—Sharon Anderson-Morgan EdD
Assistant Chief Education Officer
Special Education Unit,
Ministry of Education, Youth and Information, Jamaica

. . . . .

This is an extremely profound production. The author has covered useful areas of study for parents, teachers, educators, and Christians. This makes the content areas quite expansive, and will benefit a broad group of individuals.

—Adelle Brown, OD,
Retired Chief Education Officer
Ministry of Education, Youth and Information, Jamaica

. . . . .

This work is arresting, informative and even convicting. I thought I would simply skim through but I got hooked from the opening chapter. Reading on I saw how needed this work is for all who seek to inform groups of people (schools, religious bodies, social clubs, etc.). I kept saying to myself as I read 'Do we really know or care to know how many of the folk we seek to teach are struggling with varied disabilities, especially the children and youth?

To say this book is valuable and useful in every Caribbean country would be something of an understatement. I recommend it as necessary, to everyone, globally, who is genuinely serious about affecting the minds and lives of the people they volunteer to help or are paid to guide."

—Dr. the Rev. Clinton Chisholm
Academic Dean,
Caribbean Graduate School of Theology

. . . . .

Are you wondering how to handle kids with a behavior disorder? This book will give you insight, but most of all it will touch your heart. Because the insights Clara passes on to her readers are not only gained through study, but much more so through her own personal search and that of her co-workers: a journey with ups and downs, but fueled through an abundance of faith, love and determination. Therefore this book provides hope for children and young people with special needs, but it also provides hope for ourselves. Whatever challenge we and our loved ones face in life, it is my prayer that this book fuels your hope, so that—with the help of God and of others—you can say: 'Yes, we can!'

—Dr. Gea Gort
Missiologist and Author
Business as Mission; BAM Global Movement
Board of Regents Member, Bakke Graduate University

. . . . .

It is said that the Lord Jesus came to earth to do only three days work, that is, to die for our sins, be buried, and to rise again. So why did He spend in excess of two years of ministry immediately before that? He was engaged in the business of education, the process of optimum socialization to ensure human flourishing. He trained His disciples to care for the poor and the marginalized; he taught them how to fish for people of every stratum of society. In a word, His ministry for those years was evangelistic, therapeutic, philanthropic, but essentially didactic.

In this book Dr Clara Ricketts takes a leaf out of her Master's curriculum, and shares it with us. If Jesus showed compassion for the marginalized of His day, Dr Ricketts demonstrates, in these pages, the same kind of concern for those who need it most. The Gospels, particularly Mark's, portray the disciples as awfully slow learners, as a backdrop to the longsuffering of their Teacher. Dr Ricketts does something similar for her students in the twenty first century. Her testimony is not that of an arm-chair theologian; it is more akin to that of the Good Samaritan; that of Joseph in the book of Acts; that of the Teacher par excellence, colourfully depicted in all of the Good Book, especially the New Testament.

—Delano Vincent Palmer, ThD,
Deputy President Emeritus,
Jamaica Theological Seminary

ACKNOWLEDGEMENTS

When I first thought of converting my dissertation into a book, I expressed my desire to Dr Larry Peabody, one of my professors at Bakke Graduate University (BGU), who then referred me to Susan G. Spousta, coordinator of the BGU Publishing Team. After some preliminaries and a feeling of discouragement, Susan sought a writing coach for me in the person of Dr Gea Gort, who accepted me warmly, and began the journey with me. And what a blessing it has been as she walked with me patiently and lovingly, with no material gain for herself. Her main counsel resonated with me. She said, "Clara, write from your heart," and those words set me moving. I want to express my sincere gratitude to Larry, Susan, and most of all to you Gea. I am greatly indebted to you. I must also express my appreciation to a number of other persons who have helped to make this book a reality.

My son, Richard, has been my real motivator in the writing of this book. He would not allow me to quit even if I wanted to. I thank him for his on-going encouragement and furthermore for permitting me to expose his life experiences which provides a baseline for the message of the book.

This book would not have been possible without the support and facilitation the Board, staff, students, and parents of Sure Foundation Educational Centre which is the object of study outlined in the book. I acknowledge the pivotal role of the teachers in particular, both in the daily operation of the school and in the integral part they played in the research. Special thanks are due to Ms. Jacqueline Fagan, Ms Jennifer Mullings, and Ms Shanalee Morris who worked patiently and faithfully with me in leading the research process, and further-more, releasing their testimonies for inclusion in this book.

I take this opportunity to express my gratitude to the Special Education Unit of the Ministry of Education, and in particular to Mrs. Christina Addington, Educa-tion Officer who has offered quality support and su-pervision to the school throughout its life. By this part-nership with the Unit, I have the confidence that the content of this book is in keeping with the mandate of the Ministry of Education..

I find it useful to have a sounding board for my first rough thoughts on major issues, and my friend and colleague Mrs Vendeta Souza McKenzie fulfilled that role for me in the writing of this book. She kindly and patiently read over every chapter as I wrote them, and gave me genuine feedback on their readability and reader friendliness. I owe her a debt of gratitude .

Preparation of the manuscript for publishing was my next big challenge. I acknowledge and appreciate the kindness of Mrs Hetty de Vries who graciously under-took to edit the manuscript in a timely manner, and gave me helpful suggestions for improvement. Her help is invaluable.

Receiving feedback about the possible impact of the book was essential to my confidence in publishing the book. I sincerely thank Rev. Dr. Devon Dick and all the other persons who took the time to read the manu-script and encouraged me by their positive comments and recommendations expressed in the Endorsements and Foreword.

Finally, and most importantly, I give thanks to the Spirit of the Lord Jesus Christ who undergirded all of my work, and led the process all the way, culminating in the identification of my publisher, Extra Mile Innovators (EMI), who were willing to publish the book at affordable cost. I say thanks to EMI, while acknowledging that all the glory belong unto God.

FOREWORD

This book reminded me of the time when I was a ten-year old student of Glen Stuart Primary School Maggotty, St. Elizabeth, and I decided to close my eyes and to walk unaided from school to the principal's cottage which was 300 metres away. I knew the route very well; a path I had followed for two years. However, I tripped over a barbed wire fence and got a long cut from my knee to my ankle; a scar which I still have. It could have been worse. This incident shows that kids do the 'darndest' things, and all children need help to learn and behave properly. In fact, it can be mooted that human beings have some form of learning disabilities and display emotional behavioral disorders, and the issue is where people are in this continuum.

Therefore, the issue is really about special attention, appreciation, education, understanding and patience for children who display great amounts of disabilities and disorders and need specialized help to change for the better.

Dr. Clara Ricketts, in this seminal work, *Yes They Can: Working with Children with Learning and Behavior Disorders*, argues successfully that children with behavioral disorders and learning disabilities can be transformed into responsible and productive citizens. This parent, educator, academic and founder of a special educational school, through personal experiences and in-depth research on Christian compassion, challenges persons in government, church, school, community and homes to do better and be better in service to children with Learning Disabilities (LD) and Emotional Behavior Disorders (EBD).

Ricketts' *tour de force* is riveting, engaging, insightful and motivational. She describes her strengths, fears, opportunities and weaknesses openly and honestly, both as a classroom teacher of children with learning disabilities and behavior issues and as a parent of Richard. The real life testimonies alone make this book special, unique and a treasure trove of evidence and data concerning significant and special children. However, this study is also based on sound theory and offers practical guidelines as to the way forward. She demonstrated that through special education at her Sure Foundation Educational Centre that children could regain confidence.

Some persons have hidden hostility toward children with learning disabilities and behavioral disorders, and some parents are even embarrassed by their presence. Therefore, they blame themselves and their children in thinking that it is some 'sin' in either their lives or the children's lives why their children display LD and EBD. Children with LD and EBD have gifts and bring their talents and gifts to God's world and should be ministered to, and they also have a significant service to offer in God's mission. These children are made in the image of God and have potential to be creative and great.

Dr. Ricketts has filled a huge gap because very little if any has been documented about the nature of the challenge and opportunity to minister to these Jamaican children. Ricketts' *magnum opus* is a must read for all who want to understand the potential and possibilities in children with LD and EBD.

−Devon Dick, PhD, OD, JP
Pastor, Boulevard Baptist Church
Journalist, *The Gleaner*

ABSTRACT

This book gives the story of the writer's life experience in working with children with disabilities with specific reference to those with learning disabilities and behavior disorders. It tells of her experience both in the home setting and in the school settings but highlights the school setting. The main thrust of the book is on the work of Sure Foundation Educational Centre, a school founded by the author for the purpose of intervention for such students.

The content draws upon the doctoral research of the author which evaluated the work and impact of the school. The approaches to learning and behavior management practiced by the school are outlined for the benefit of parents, teachers and other interested persons such as students in colleges and seminaries. It details strategies which have proven to be effective as evidenced by students' outcome and the testimonies of children, parents and teachers.

Furthermore, it outlines and encourages partnerships and collaboration among parents, teachers, the church, the community and the government to help bring out the best in these children. Finally, it gives an appeal for attention to these children with learning and behavior challenges, with the conviction that they can succeed and become productive and contributing members of society, given the necessary support.

TABLE OF CONTENTS

Introduction 1
Part 1: The Children 7
  Chapter 1: My Story 9
  Chapter 2: Meet the Children 17
  Chapter 3: Their Life Experiences 27
  Chapter 4: Point of Need 35
Part 2: Intervention 49
  Chapter 5: Sure Foundation Educational Centre ... 51
  Chapter 6: The Way We Work—Teaching &
    Learning 57
  Chapter 7: The Way We Work—Behavior
    Management 69
Part 3: Impact 81
  Chapter 8: An Appreciative Inquiry 83
  Chapter 9: Student Outcome 95
Part 4: Partnership 103
  Chapter 10: The Place of Parents 105
  Chapter 11: The Place of Teachers 121
  Chapter 12: Place of the Church 133
  Chapter 13: Community Involvement 147
  Chapter 14: The Role of Government 159
  Conclusion: Doing What They Want to Do 169
About the Author 177
References 179
Appendix A: Students' Daily Record 183
Appendix B: AI Interview Guide 185
Appendix C: SFEC AI Provocative Statements 189

INTRODUCTION

As I walked in the supermarket one day, a young man came running up to me and embraced me. I looked in his face, and in fact, he was not so young after all. I stepped away and took a second look at him, and he signed to me, "Remember me?" Yes, of course I remembered him, although he had taken on some age. He was now in his late thirties, and I had him in school up to the age of seventeen. What struck me about him was his deportment as a well-groomed and purposeful gentleman. I said to him in sign language, "Is this you, Anthony (not his real name), the same Anthony who gave so much trouble at school?" He was one of the most disruptive and rebellious students in school, and one to be feared. Most persons saw him as a gang leader, who would end up as a terror to the nation until he died or was killed. Further conversation with him revealed that he was holding an honest job, lived in a stable relationship and had one daughter about twelve years old, who was standing beside him. He proudly introduced us.

On another occasion, I was invited to the wedding of Michael, a young man in my own family, who was known as extremely disobedient and unmanageable. He had violent outbursts creating damages to property and causing emotional and physical injury to family and others. He was a victim of Attention Deficit Hyper-active Disorder (ADHD), although the family did not know this at the beginning. Following appropriate intervention in his teen years, he had developed into a calm, controlled and responsible adult holding a managerial position at work. Now, he was about to take up his role as husband and father.

Can children with behavior and learning disorders be transformed to develop into responsible, productive and contributing citizens? Yes, They Can. In my journey, I have seen many more children like Anthony and Michael, who were prophesied as hopeless, and who have defied all prophesies and turned out to be successful productive men and women. Therefore, we must be careful how we treat these struggling children. We must see them and treat them according to what they can be rather than what they appear to be.

God's plan for humanity is inclusive of all people. His love extends to all people, and likewise his expectations from each person is without partiality. The Bible's position on the care and ministry to the vulnerable or those on the margins of society is very clear. References abound throughout the Bible drawing attention to the lost, the least and the last. I have related to several students with special needs, who received not only numerous suspensions but repeated expulsions from schools because of problems associated with their disabilities. Jesus has a plan for them, as He has for every human being.

In Jamaica, many of these children have been excluded from the regular school system because of their intolerable behavior. Others are out of school, because their parents can find no suitable placements for them in the public school system, and they cannot afford the cost of private special education programs. And then there are children who are in special education facilities, which are under-developed because of financial constraints. Yet, if these children are left without appropriate intervention, they have the potential of diverting their behaviors towards criminal activities, thereby threatening the security of the nation and destroying their own lives.

There tends to be constant complaints about these children who present a problem to the school system and society. Then, because of their intellectual limitations, these children are not perceived as persons who can add significantly to the national economy, while at the same time requiring so much for education. This means that the inflow far exceeds the potential outflow, and this imbalance does not make them a priority in our society for financial support.

Moreover, the disabilities relating to learning and behavior—especially behavior—are invisible and so fail to attract empathy or understanding received by the more visible forms, such as physical and sensory disabilities. Therefore plans for the disability sector often do not include these children. They are misfits. Meanwhile, they abhor themselves and suffer silently. Neither do they want to be identified with disabled persons. They have special needs but are hesitant in accessing support, even when such support is available. Still, their need for help is great.

The objective of this book is to unveil the vulnerability of children with Learning Disabilities (LD) and Emotional Behavior Disorders (EBD) and reveal ways in which significant persons can make a difference in their lives. The thesis is that, given the opportunity, all children irrespective of their disabilities can be achievers and positive productive citizens of society. It draws upon the experience of Sure Foundation Educational Centre (SFEC), a non-profit, non-governmental Christian organization operating in the city of Kingston, Jamaica, and serving children of secondary school age with LD and EBD. Further information about the school is outlined in Chapter 5, Sure Foundation Educational Centre.

The book is presented in four parts. Part 1 gives an introduction to the children about whom I write. It consists of four chapters outlining my own experience with children with special needs at home and at school, presenting samples of the children of SFEC, their life experiences, and their real needs.

Part 2 deals with intervention for these children. It is presented in three chapters giving information about the school, and how we work covering learning strategies and behavior management skills.

Part 3 focusses on results and confirming that the students can achieve. This section outlines part of my doctoral research in the school and the outcome. It is presented in Part 2 two chapters including an Appreciative Inquiry of the impact of the school and the outcome of the students going through the school programme.

The final section, Part 4, highlights the collaborative support necessary to help the students maximize their potentials. There are five chapters in this section targeting parents, teachers, the church, the community and the government. Each of these groups are encouraged to do their part to help these children with special needs accomplish their God-given purpose on earth.

I hope that as you read this book, you will gain a better understanding of the true condition of these children and the challenges they face. Furthermore, I hope that the book will help you to recognize them and consider ways in which you can help them to grow into productive and contributing members of society. Finally, I pray that the contents of this book will spark your interest in some way.

PART 1:
THE CHILDREN

CHAPTER 1:
MY STORY

INVOLVEMENT WITH SPECIAL NEEDS CHILDREN AND ADOLESCENTS

I was introduced to children with special needs early in my teaching career, and I have continued on that path for over four decades. Working with children, youth and adults during this time constitutes my most significant experience both at home and at work. I learned tremendous lessons along the way and continue to do so.

A RUDE AWAKENING

After leaving teachers' college, I taught grade-one students in the primary school for three years with large classes. The brilliant children at the top of the stream gave me much pleasure as well as the children of average ability. However, there were always the few students who found their places at the back of the class, and who seemed to leave at the end of the year at the same low academic level at which they entered. I was always concerned about these children, but I could not help them because of my large class size of 60-70 students each year.

Therefore, when a colleague told me about a school for deaf children with class sizes of no more than ten students, I perceived it as the perfect job for me. Their disability was not a deterrent. I reasoned that with ten students in a class, I could make them learn irrespective of any type of disability. Shortly after, they told me of a vacancy at the school, and I applied for the job. At the interview my exuberance was clear. I boldly told the interviewers that if I was not selected, then I would apply again whenever another vacancy occurred. I got the job.

However, I was in for a rude awakening. On the first day of the job, I got a class of nine 9-10 year old students. The class consisted of eight boys and one girl. The principal said, "This is your class" and left. I stepped into the room, and no one looked at me.

They were all busy conversing among themselves with gestures, signs, and speech which was meaningless to me. No matter what I did to get their attention, they simply ignored me. By the end of the day, I was tired, completely frustrated and distressed. On my way home, I bought a colouring book and crayons with the hope of attracting their attention the following day. Still in my pain and frustration upon reaching home, I slept from 4:00 p.m. until the next morning.

The next day, I pulled the book apart, gave a sheet to each student and made crayons available to all. They still did not look at me, but they engaged themselves in the activity, finished it in a short time, and then returned to their own affairs.

I questioned myself, "What do I do next?"

I remembered that all children love physical education; so I decided to take them outside. That decision was a mistake. They ran over the entire compound, paying no attention to me. They were profoundly deaf, so they could not hear me if I tried to call them.

After running after them and much struggle to get them inside, one of the experienced teachers said to me, "You have to let them know that you are in control." I took her advice, and when there seemed to be no other alternative, I slapped one of them to declare my authority.

That action was another mistake. They all rebelled in the most outrageous way, lifting up the desks and chairs and throwing them down, pointing in my face and making incomprehensible utterances. Now I was in real trouble. I remembered how convincing I had been at the interview, but then I had not envisioned a behavioral problem coupled with the disability.

My real experience in special education began on the third day with this class of predominantly deaf boys. On that day, I was forced to find a way to get their attention, because I could not accept the notion of failure and disappointment from those who had put enough trust in me to offer me the job. That evening after the students rebelled against me, as I struggled for a solution, it occurred to me that I needed to appeal to their sense of vision. I looked for the most colourful dress in my wardrobe and matching shoes. I made a chart to introduce my first lesson, and name tags for the students' desks. The next morning, I arrived at school extremely early, rearranged the classroom, and labelled the students' desks with their names. I took my position at the entrance of the building to meet the students.

When the first student arrived, he looked at my dress and began to match the colour of his shirt with a colour in my dress, by pointing to each one consecutively. Next, he drew the attention of his approaching friend and directed him to my dress with similar matching gestures. The school did not wear uniforms then, so the students' clothes varied in style and colours. Their gazes caught my shoes, and they became excited about some flaps on my shoes and started to play with them. I held my breath and said in my heart, *Thank the Lord; they are looking at me.*

Soon the whole class was around me, and I was the centre of attention. I quickly capitalized on this privilege and led them to the classroom.

In the classroom, their eyes popped open, because the room was different and they did not know where to sit. They looked at me again for directions. I began to point out their name tags to them, until they were all seated. Now I felt in control, so I pulled out my next tool, the chart, which was the month's calendar written in big and bold letters on a colourful sheet of cartridge paper.

While I explained the concepts of 'yesterday' and 'today' using demonstrations, as well as the chart, they were fully attentive. Afterwards, I gestured to ask their opinion of where on the wall to place the chart. They all eagerly made suggestions by pointing to different areas on the wall. Now I had their attention and needed to keep it, so I introduced copy writing, doing one letter at a time to force them to look in my direction each time to get the next letter to copy. At this point, I sighed in relief, recognizing that I had begun to teach. This is when I began my long career in special education, some of which I have shared with you in this book.

A FAMILY EXPERIENCE

After learning to cope in a challenging school environment with deaf children, and some years later, I was encouraged to adopt a child from one of the nation's children's homes. I had accompanied a friend to the court for the adoption of her baby, whom she had in foster care. At the end of the session, the adoption officer said to me, "Wouldn't you like to adopt one of our little boys? We have so many of them who need to be adopted, and I know one who would be just right for you." Most of the children who were adopted were girls including the one of my friend. The boys were left behind, so I gave thought to the appeal of the adoption officer, followed through, and finally took the child she had suggested into foster care. He was two years old.

When I took him to church, someone commented, "He is so hyperactive." It is true that he had been running all over the place, back and forth, but I was offended because someone was labelling my child. Furthermore, at the first nursery school he attended at two years old, the teachers labelled him "bad boy." I was livid. They were labelling a two-year-old child as 'bad.' What would become of him, I asked myself. I moved him from that facility to a pre-school. By this time, he was three years old and creating much havoc with his disruptive behavior. Some teachers were patient with him. Others tolerated him until he completed a year there.

I had to take the major responsibility to monitor his behavior both at home and school. Meanwhile, he was making no progress academically. At four years old, hef was diagnosed as having severe Attention Deficit Hyperactive Disorder (ADHD) and had to be placed on medication during school days in order to survive there. The medication kept him fairly quiet for approximately four hours each morning, but by early afternoon, he was back to disruptive behavior. In addition, his psycho-educational assessment revealed that he had learning disabilities which would retard his rate of learning.

All of his schooling was done in private settings, because there were no public facilities catering to his needs. Even then, my work of monitoring him at school was a full time task. I had to do my part while encouraging his teachers, because I did not want him to get excluded from school. I resolved within myself then that I would start a school for children like him.

His first six years at school from pre-school to preparatory school were wasted because no learning took place. Eventually, I was introduced to a special education programme just being birthed, providing the small group setting and individual attention which he needed. It was in that programme that he learnt to read at the age of nine.

RISE TO LEADERSHIP

Three years after beginning my journey at the school for the deaf, having received certification and some experience, I was appointed teacher-in-charge of the school. Eventually I moved into the position of principal, when the school gained autonomy. The major challenge in working with deaf children was communication. Next in line were the behavior problems. My responsibility was to guide the teachers in this process while assuming the role as dean of discipline. The necessity for parent conferences became a regular part of my daily activities. Later, I moved on to being principal at the secondary school, and the challenge of behavior management continued with greater gravity among the teenagers.

My son came to me while I was in this job, and I began to understand what it meant to be sitting in the parents' seat in a parent-teacher conference. What a revelation that was. I was operating in the dual position of being both teacher and parent of children with disabilities including behavior disorders. I read much and applied behavioral theories at home, but it was more difficult to implement these at school, because the full cooperation of teachers was necessary but challenging to maintain in a large setting. This reality intensified my resolution to start a school of my own with smaller numbers and more opportunity for direct involvement in the daily lives of the students. This resolution gave rise to the birth of Sure Foundation Educational Centre.

I know first-hand the struggles and frustrations of working with a child with learning and behavior disorders in a classroom setting and in a family setting. It is from this vantage point that I share with you in this book.

CHAPTER 2:
MEET THE CHILDREN

One may ask the questions, "What kind of children are these? What is wrong with them, that they should deserve special consideration or favour?" When children are disobedient or disruptive, you punish them and let them know who is in charge. That is all there is to it.

Normally, you will recognize them first by their behavior. Unlike the person whose physical disability captures your attention, it is the behavior of these children which first attracts your attention. This is so whether you meet them in the market place, at home or in school.

Here is a sample of the children within my experience at Sure Foundation Educational Centre. They are all teenagers ranging from 13 to 17 years old. Their real names have been concealed for privacy. In some of these cases, it is the behavior that is most prominent and in some it is learning disability that comes to the fore. Still in others, it is the social factor that is the most over-riding, although all cases have social-emotional factors embedded.

ANDREW (LEARNING DISABILITY)

Andrew lives with both mother and father. He has one older and one younger brother, who are both brilliant. Prior to coming to SFEC, he had been excluded from several schools because of stubborn behavior.

At his present school, Andrew exhibits stubborn behaviors sometimes, but at other times, he is cooperative and talkative, reaching out to his teachers for love and understanding. His disposition is sometimes sad, and he is easily angered, though not disrespectful to his teachers. At the same time, he adores his parents, especially his father, and hungers for their approval above everything else.

He does very little work and only when he wishes to do so. When he does decide to work, he does so very slowly and so hardly ever completes given assignments. He is strong in the areas of reasoning, religious knowledge and verbal expression, but he has challenges in spelling, mathematics, reading, comprehension and writing. At age sixteen, he is performing several grades below his expected level.

MARCEL (BEHAVIOR)

Marcel lives with his paternal grandmother in an extended family setting including aunts, uncles and cousins. He has several siblings living with his mother for whom he carries intense feelings of hate and anger.

These emotions are carried over into the school. He gets angry easily, and when he does, he is out of control of himself. He seeks to dominate both students and teachers. He demands attention always and insists on having his own way. He reasons deeply, but his reasoning is irrational and always leans to rationalization of his inappropriate behaviors. He is impulsive, focuses on his school work for only short periods of time, and is often disrespectful to teachers.

He leads the rest of the school by his very presence. Almost all of the students in the school revere and depend on him to support them in their own wrong behavior. Meanwhile he is friendly to teachers at most times and extremely helpful. However, he gets into serious conflict with any student who opposes him. Sometimes he even equates himself with teachers and challenges their authority

JASON (BEHAVIOR)

Jason lives alone with his father in a volatile community. He is boisterous, strong-willed, and disruptive. He rebels against anything that appears to be unjust in his eyes, and gets into uncontrollable rage. He is extremely disobedient, uses indecent language, smokes marijuana and is not afraid to challenge adults. He is disrespectful to parents, teachers and adults generally.

Prior to being accepted at SFEC, he had been excluded from three previous schools. At this new school, he strives to be a leader, and consistently challenges the established student leader. He is big for his age, and tends to intimidate other students with his size.

Meanwhile, he is extremely caring and helpful to both students and teachers. He is interested in learning, but he has difficulties in the key areas of mathematics and language arts. He talks incessantly and is inattentive, despite the fact that he wants to learn. He admits to his short-comings and pledges to change repeatedly, but in his own words, he finds it difficult to do so.

RENALDO (LEARNING DISABILITY / ASPERGER'S SYNDROME)

Renaldo is a quiet student fixed in his own ways and beliefs. He lives with his mother and siblings in a volatile community, but expresses no fear. He is observant, thinks deeply and readily distinguishes between acceptable and unacceptable behavior. He overtly objects to the wrong and rebellious behaviors of others and is not afraid to speak out against them.

On the other hand, he is rigid in his ways. He is inflexible both in behavior and opinions, but he has strong reasoning powers, even if he is sometimes irrational.

He has learning challenges in mathematics and spelling but is strong in reading and comprehension. He also has a memory problem which affects his progress in mathematics. He will learn the concept well and, with his reasoning ability, readily deciphers mathematical problems but, without constant practice and over-learning, he just as quickly forgets the rules.

JERRY (BEHAVIOR)

Jerry is the second of two children and lives with his paternal grandparents. He is disobedient and is involved in extreme misconduct both at home and on the street.

At school he constantly displays disruptive behavior. He gets angry easily, becomes abusive and uses threatening language. He is vengeful and does not seem to care when disciplined. He makes verbal commitments to trying and shows attempts at doing so, but this is often short-lived. He admits to his wrong doing only when pressured to do so. He lies constantly, never admits to his wrong behavior and, when convicted, he blames others for it. He frequently gets into fights both at school and on the road. He is rebellious, negative in thought and aggressive. He attaches himself to the wrong company on the streets that speak and practice illegal behavior including the use of weapons. Whenever he gets angry, he is uncontrollable and appears to be dangerous.

Meanwhile, his academic performance is always below expected standards. His learning is affected by hyperactivity, inattention and a mind that always seems to be wandering. Even when speaking to him individually, it is difficult to attract his attention. His mind always seems to be somewhere else. Yet he sometimes presents himself as a warm, friendly and caring child easy to love.

NOEL (BEHAVIOR)

Noel lives with only his mother. He is extremely hyperactive, has a short attention span, is impulsive, aggressive, argumentative, oppositional, defiant, talkative and has no respect for authority. These characteristics have resulted in constant disruptive behavior. On more than one occasion, he got into a rage and had to be strongly restrained to avoid serious damage to him-self, others and the school property.

He was expelled from more than one school prior to coming to SFEC. He declares that he trusts no one and does not care about anything, including school. He constantly challenges teachers and has sought to fight them on more than one occasion. Meanwhile he rebels against his family situation.

His behavior is constantly disruptive to the entire school. In addition, he weaves himself among the students and secretly engages them in unacceptable behaviors. He speaks any negative thing that comes to his mind including expletives in an undertone during class time. He knows that his behavior is un-acceptable, and he seems to take pride in this. He has only a few learning challenges, but his academic per-formance is hampered by his negative and disruptive behavior.

TERRY (LEARNING DISABILITY)

Terry lives in an uptown, middle-income home with her maternal aunt and step uncle while her mother lives abroad. She has difficulty in her academic work—particularly in the areas of comprehension and math-ematics—accompanied by memory deficiency and mental disorganization.

She is overly sensitive, and this sometimes leads to interpersonal challenges. Otherwise, she exhibits no behavior problems. She is purposeful and has a posit-ive attitude towards work. She tries hard constantly and compensates for her memory and organizational deficiencies by rigid physical organization of her materials. She makes notes in detail and keeps them in date order for the entire year, constantly referring to them as needed. She keeps these as her learning crutch but is inflexible in extending her thoughts beyond these.

She is a role model in conduct—disciplined, responsible and conscientious—giving good leadership and rising to the office of head girl. She is undeterred by the disruptive behavior of the other students, holding firm in maintaining her own standards and never failing to correct the other children.

ABIGAIL (LEARNING DISABILITY AND SOCIAL FACTORS)

Abigail lives with her paternal grandmother. Her other siblings live with her mother. She is usually very sociable but easily over-extends herself to strangers and has an over-riding desire to please.

She has unusual emotions and sometimes cries and throws a tantrum when she is told 'no' about what she wants to do. She demonstrates both physical and verbal aggression when she does not get her way and finds it difficult to fit in with her peers.

She is immature for her age and simple in her behavior. She is limited in her thinking capacity and finds it difficult to understand social concepts. Her schoolmates set her apart as 'handicapped' and call her names accordingly, thereby inciting more aggression from her.

ALRICK (LEARNING DISABILITY)

Alrick resides with his mother and siblings, and there is good interpersonal relationships within the family. Little is known of the part his father plays in his life.

At age 12, his reading recognition and comprehension skills are far below his age level. He also has significant problems in mathematics and spelling accompanied by poor memory. His challenges come to the fore when he has to concentrate on specific concepts or discipline his mind to move along established paths. However, he has good verbal reasoning and oral expression.

In school, he is easily distracted and restless. His behavior problems are subtle. He constantly expresses dissatisfaction with his placement in a special school and feels himself superior to other children, whose disabilities are more pronounced than his.

FRANCINE (LEARNING DISABILITY/AUTISM)

Francine lives with only her mother. At age eighteen, she hardly makes an attempt to speak, and when she does, it is in an angry tone and mostly unintelligible.

At school, she stays by herself, does not socialize at any time and insists on doing only what pleases her. She attaches herself to one teacher, constantly follows that one, does assignments given to her and projects herself as being lost whenever that teacher is absent.

In addition to problems in communication, her writing is illegible, and she makes little attempt at oral reading. She becomes stuck in mathematical concepts unable to go much beyond simple calculations in the four operations.

COMMONALITIES

The children described are from various home settings; there are some things that are common among them in the midst of all their differences. For some, it is behavior propelled by social factors (Marcel, Jason). For some, the dominant factor is behavior, although social factors are not excluded (Jerry, Noel). For others, it is behavior associated with the kind of learning disability (Renaldo, Francine). Still for others, it is social factors and learning disability (Andrew, Abigail). To a lesser extent, learning disability is the sole challenge. (Terry, Alrick)

An outstanding feature among all those who have a behavior component is anger and aggression. It is also noteworthy that seventy percent (70%) of these children are living in families led by women. Only ten percent (10%) of the children live in a structured nuclear family. In a study done on the total demographics of parenting in the school, it was found that fifty-three percent (53%) of the students lived with their mother only, and altogether eighty-seven percent (87%) lived with female heads—mother, grandmother or aunt (Ricketts, Williams & Worges, 2012). Broken families and female dominant leadership in the home are common features.

CHAPTER 3:
THEIR LIFE EXPERIENCES

In Jamaica, a number of under-achievers have dropped out of the regular school system either because they are demotivated or school authorities have excluded them because of behavior challenges. The disability of these children is invisible. Consequently, they do not attract the same empathy as do the visible forms of disability. Therefore, they suffer inwardly, while attracting negative reactions from the outside, and are poised to be twice defeated in the race of life, unless they receive the necessary help and support.

The students of Sure Foundation Educational Centre (SFEC) have been the victims of various circumstances and experiences that militate against them. What follows is a sample of their situations including factors that classify as abuse in more than one way.

FAMILY DYSFUNCTIONALITY

Most of the children described are negatively impacted by family situations over which they have no control. One must be cognizant of the fact that the family is the first and primary agent of socialization.

It follows that the family to a great extent determines how one perceives oneself. The role of the parent is often described as most crucial in the development of the total personality of a child. "Parents are an integral part of the first community which the child inhabits, and they help him to formulate his first conceptions of himself as a good/bad, capable/incapable individual" (Hyman-Anglin 2006, 59-60). This aspect of socialization penetrates the school system and influences childrens' academic performance to a great extent. In this way, distinction between academic abilities begin to appear between those children who are socialized to believe that they have high competencies and those who are socialized to believe that they have low competencies.

There are often underlying forces within the family that negatively influence the behavior of the children. Marcel's case is a typical example.

He experienced extreme violence in his family from infancy, which changed the course of his life. His father was killed by a maternal family member. When he was old enough to understand what had happened, his anger began to flare and he resolved to kill someone in return. His paternal family nurtured him and sought counsel for him. However, he developed other emotional side effects, was constantly in fights at school, which resulted in his exclusion. At SFEC, he confessed his inner struggles, like Paul, wanting to do good, but the impact of his father's death continually resonates with him. He is afraid that the anger will eventually overcome him and conclude in murder.

Marcel is a confused child. Every part of him is crying out for help. To simply punish him for his outbursts of anger would drive him further towards rebellion and revenge.

EMOTIONAL AND PSYCHOLOGICAL ABUSE

Emotional and psychological abuse in children has been defined as behaviors, speech, and actions of parents, caregivers, or other significant figures in a child's life that have a negative mental impact on the child. By this definition, Marcel's case could be classified as child abuse by the actions of his parent. He did not witness the physical or emotional abuse of his parents to each other, but in so far as their action has a negative mental impact on him, he is the victim of abuse. And so he cries for help.

Jason's father, with whom he lives at thirteen years old, is rarely at home. After school, Jason walks up and down the streets, plays in the streets with his friends, visits the library and makes trouble there, or hangs out at a bike shop in the community, which, he says, helps to keep him out of trouble.

When he does go home, he manages himself, buys food at the nearby shop, over-eats, then joins company in the community to smoke ganja. He does no homework. Since his father is rarely home, they may or may not see each other for the evening. In the morning, Jason dresses sloppily for school, stops at the shop on his way and buys fast food for breakfast. He is a child growing up without parental guidance.

SEXUAL AND VERBAL ABUSE

Other children struggle with life experiences and abuse attracted to them because of their low functioning level. Abusive adults inside and outside of the family target them, because they reason that the children are too low in intelligence to understand what is happening or to report it. Such is the case of Abigail, who was first sexually assaulted by her stepfather at the age of ten. Her paternal grandmother took her for refuge from her mother, who still lived with the man who molested Abigail. By age fourteen, she was molested by two other men. Consequently, in addition to her social and intellectual challenges, she had to cope with the emotional trauma of attending the courts periodically over an extended period of time and reliving her experiences each time.

At home, she is over-protected by her grandmother, who constantly worries about her safety. Meanwhile, she must live under the verbal abuse of her great-grandmother, who constantly uses indecent language to her and taunts her about her low academic achievement.

At school, Abigail is a confused child. She is open about her home affairs and seeks every opportunity to relay her distress to her teachers. She worries about everything and everyone in her family life, always seeking attention and often does so from the wrong sources. She is over-friendly with boys and male staff, goes overboard to do favors for them and is tickled by the slightest attention from any of them. Her cry for help is loud and great!

Abigail is the victim of sexual and verbal abuse struggling to establish appropriate social and emotional relationships with family, friends and care-givers. Meanwhile, her hunger for warm relationships has the potential to drive her into a further vulnerable position. Furthermore, her concentration on these extraneous factors negatively impacts her progress in school.

REJECTION

Because Learning Disability (LD) and Emotional Behavioral Disorder (EBD) are closely linked, some of these children experience rejection because of their low academic performance, their behavior or both. While rejection is a common part of life, this type of rejection is more deliberate and difficult to cope with than others. This child is likely to be rejected at home as well as at school, but the greater impact stems from rejection at home. This is the place where a child needs to feel accepted and wanted regardless of what the rest of the world thinks about him. Home is his place of refuge from the terrors of the world. So the child who is rejected at home is in great pain and turmoil. The case of Andrew is an example.

Although living in a stable nuclear family, Andrew is in a place of rejection. His two brothers are brilliant, and his parents fail to accept that he has a disability. They believe that his low performance in school is a result of his stubbornness. Therefore, they set out to beat the stubbornness out of him. He is rejected by both parents to different degrees. His father, who is the pastor of his church, physically abuses him under the guise of following the Scriptures, for example, Pro-verbs 23:13-14, which instructs parents to beat the child and save his soul from Hell.

His mother abuses him mentally by flooding his mind with criticisms and comparing him with his younger brother. Consequently, Andrew developed re-sentment against this younger brother and attempts to abuse him, thereby fueling the anger of the rest of the family, which leads to further rejection and abuse. A vicious cycle ensues.

Many children like Andrew are anxious to please their parents and be accepted by them, but they exper-ience only rejection and feelings of helplessness. One can understand the depth of Andrew's pain, as he craves acceptance from his own family.

A child who has few or no friends may feel rejected by peers. At school, Andrew is a loner. He finds it diffi-cult to maintain relationships with his peers, as he is always striving to prove himself superior to them in conversations. At the same time, he finds it difficult to focus on his school work and succeed. Therefore, he is in social isolation both at home and at school, and this situation further negatively affects his achievement at school. His countenance reflects a stressed and un-happy child. His cry for help is great.

INJURED SELF-ESTEEM

Many students with disabilities suffer from low self-esteem, which is defined as the degree to which we feel confident, consider ourselves valuable and respect ourselves. Self-esteem is learnt in childhood, and certain experiences may interfere with its development, such as being subjected to criticism from parents and caregivers. Non-acceptance of children's disabilities on the part of parents—as in the case of Andrew—can also lead to the injured self-esteem of these children. Other factors experienced by children with LD and EBD include the following:

- social isolation
- self-doubt
- suppressed anger against parents
- feelings of inadequacy
- missing out on experiences that would foster a sense of confidence and purpose
- receiving little or no positive reinforcement for accomplishments
- being stigmatized for unusual appearance or behaviors

Kevin is a ward of the state living in a children's home. He was abandoned by his parents in infancy. In the home, house mothers change periodically, and he never seems to be with one long enough to develop a bond. Each mother complains of Kevin's poor conduct, including stealing and lying..

At school, Kevin is strongly criticized by his peers and accused of being girlish. He clings to his teachers for support and readily informs them of offences created by other students. However, among his peers, he is timid and withdrawn. He cannot identify with the family life experiences that the other students share, and this gives him a feeling of isolation. He accepts the fact that they do not like him and tries to protect himself from them, especially after he has made a complaint against them. He attempts to gain recognition for himself by out-doing his class in speed for mathematical calculations, but he often makes several errors in the process.

At the age of 16 years, he repeatedly speaks negatively about himself and expresses no plans or expectations for his life. His response to every question about his future is, "I don't know," while his expression seems to say, "I don't care."

Chapter 4:
Point of Need

General behavioral issues applicable to all children will be partly responsible for the absence of appropriate responses in learning and behavior. However, it is also true that in many cases there are special factors in the lives of these children which make it extremely difficult if not impossible for them to respond appropriately, despite the fact that they want to do so. These include a range of biological, social and emotional factors. Biological factors include their brain function, which determines their capacity for learning. Social factors include their family and environmental situations over which they have no control. Emotional factors include their coping skills from the impact of their experiences. These various factors bring children into various kinds of needs.

The classification of children with special needs is one that has been the subject of much debate. It is a complex issue involving emotional, political and humane considerations in addition to scientific and educational interests. There are 13 categories of special education as defined by the Individuals with Disabilities Education

Act (IDEA). We will focus on those disabilities which fall within our observation among the students who are the concern of this book. The children of SFEC display characteristics of the broad category of Learning Disabilities (LD) and Emotional Behavioual Disorders (EBD) to a large extent, and Pervasive Developmental Disorders (PDD) to a lesser extent.

LEARNING DISABILITIES (LD)

Learning disabilities are neurologically-based processing problems. These problems can interfere with learning basic skills such as reading, writing and/or math. They can also interfere with higher level skills such as organization, time planning, abstract reasoning, long or short term memory and attention. It is important to realize that learning disabilities can affect an individual's life beyond academics and impact relationships with family, friends and co-workers in the workplace.

Generally speaking, people with learning disabilities are of average or above average intelligence. There often appears to be a gap between the potential and actual achievement of the individual. This is why learning disabilities are referred to as "hidden disabilities": These persons look perfectly "normal" and seem to be very bright and intelligent people, yet they may be unable to demonstrate the skill level expected from someone else of a similar age.

A learning disability cannot be cured or fixed; it is a lifelong challenge. However, with appropriate support and intervention, people with learning disabilities can achieve success in school, work, relationships and the community. Each student of SFEC displays one or more of the sub-categories of LD outlined below.

DYSCALCULIA

Dyscalculia is a specific learning disability that affects a person's ability to understand numbers and learn math facts. This type of learning disability involves difficulty with calculating numbers or grasping math concepts. Individuals with this type of LD may also have poor comprehension of math symbols, may struggle with memorizing and organizing numbers, have difficulty telling time or have trouble with counting. There is no single type of math disability, as it varies from child to child. Almost all students of SFEC display some type of dyscalculia.

DYSGRAPHIA

Dysgraphia is a specific learning disability that affects a person's handwriting and fine motor skills. Problems may include illegible handwriting, inconsistent spacing, poor spatial planning on paper, poor spelling and or difficulty composing writing as well as thinking and writing at the same time. This type of LD is strongly evident in at least one student in school at the time of writing.

DYSLEXIA

This is a specific learning disability that affects reading and related language-based processing skills. The severity can differ in each individual but can affect reading fluency, decoding, reading comprehension, recall, writing, spelling, sometimes speech and can exist along with other related disorders. Dyslexia is sometimes referred to as a Language-Based Learning Disability. Almost all students passing through the doors of SFEC experience dyslexia.

SHORT AND LONG TERM MEMORY PROBLEMS

Many of our students suffer from poor memory. They have trouble remembering facts, numbers and assignments. They also have difficulty following instructions.

Three types of memory are important to learning. Working memory, short-term memory and long-term memory are used in the processing of both verbal and non-verbal information. If there are deficits in any or all of these types of memory, the ability to store and retrieve information required to carry out tasks can be impaired.

PERVASIVE DEVELOPMENTAL DISORDERS (PDD)

Autism and Asperger Syndrome are the two Pervasive Developmental Disorders that receive the majority of media coverage. Characteristics of PDD include sensory difficulties, repetitive behavior, cognitive impairment, social impairment and immune deficiencies. In Chapter 2, I introduced Renaldo, who exhibits some degree of cognitive and social impairment and so falls in this category.

AUTISM

Characteristics of Autism vary widely, but common early signs include the following:

1. Non-typical eye-contact, lack of visual tracking, disengagement of visual attention.
2. Prolonged latency to disengage visual attention.
3. Alternating pattern of extreme passivity and extreme distress reactions.
4. Tendency to fixate on particular objects in the environment.
5. Decreased expression of positive affection.
6. Delayed expressive and receptive language.
7. Lack of orientating to name.
8. Lack of imitation, social smiling, social interest.
9. Lack of affect and sensory-oriented behaviors.

There are many types of autism. Classic autism is the most commonly understood of the autism spectrum disorders. People with classic autism often have a great deal of trouble interacting with others, strong sensory issues, health problems and developmental delays. Within the life of the school, we have accommodated a few students displaying some of these characteristics. Francine is one such student (see Chapter 2). She has a big problem interacting with others, lacks affect and sensory-related behaviors, and has delays in expressive and receptive language.

ASPERGER SYNDROME

Kids with Asperger Syndrome often find it very stressful to meet new people. Many persons view someone with Asperger Syndrome as having a difference rather than a disability.

STRENGTHS AND CHALLENGES OF A STUDENT WITH ASPERGER SYNDROME

STRENGTHS	CHALLENGES
Honest	Making friends
Determined	Managing feelings
An expert	Taking advice
Kind	Handwriting
Speaks his/her mind	Knowing when someone is thinking
Enjoys solitude	Being teased or bullied
Perfectionist	Showing as much affection as others expect
Reliable friend	Switching tasks
Good at Art	Changing environments
Liked by adults	Varying approaches and strategies

Source: *Different Brains, Different Learners: How to Reach the Hard to Reach* by Eric Jensen, 2010.

The behavior of student Renaldo more strongly resembles Asperger Syndrome. To a large extent, he is honest, not afraid to speak his mind, enjoys solitude, has problems taking advice, switching tasks and changing environment. At the time of writing, his ability at art began to be pronounced.

EMOTIONAL BEHAVIORAL DISORDERS (EBD)

Teachers have a high tolerance for a student who uses a wheelchair and who needs extra help in physical education classes, because this student has a visible disability. However, since the nature of an emotional and behavioral disability can manifest itself in difficult, disruptive and aggressive behavior, most people do not react sympathetically. It is vital to understand that the latter student has a disability with which he/she is struggling. This student's brain is wired in a way that results in maladaptive, irrational behavior in moments of anger, frustration and anxiety.

What we want to emphasize is that some students in our classrooms can't rather than won't behave optimally. It is not the fault of these students, and they should be thought of in an empathic way.

In his book *Severe Behavior Problems*, prominent behavior analyst Mark Durand categorizes all human behaviors as being motivated by four functions: to get attention, to escape or avoid something, to gain something tangible like an object, or to get some sensory (smell, taste, feel) satisfaction. (Minahan 2012, Loc. 310).

Students who are stuck can be bossy (even bullying), can insist everything go their way, may not take turns well, and can be easily frustrated, hard to negotiate with, or demanding. (Minahan, 2012) Most of the students of SFEC display characteristics of EBD as well as LD. They have one or more learning disabilities coupled with one or more behavior disorders. The most outstanding EBD displayed are Attention Deficit Hyperactive Disorder, Oppositional Defiant Disorder and Conduct Disorder.

ATTENTION DEFICIT HYPERACTIVE DISORDER (ADHD)

ADHD as a disability may find its place among learning disabilities as well as behavioral disorders, but since it is the behavior that most often gets the attention of people, I chose to include it in this category of disabilities. Since all types of learning disabilities affect how a child performs in school, sometimes they can develop emotional or behavioral issues.

It is a disorder that includes difficulty in staying focused and paying attention, controlling behavior and hyperactivity. Research indicates that 30-50 percent of children with ADHD also have a specific learning disability, and the two conditions can interact to make learning extremely challenging. This is definitely the case with the population at SFEC.

Children with ADHD often need more structure than other children and clearer instruction as to what kinds of behavior an adult expects . Praise and opportunities for a positive relationship with parents and/or teachers are powerful tools for managing disruptive behavior, which tends to escalate when a relationship is mostly negative interactions. For this reason, we strive to maintain a positive environment at SFEC.

These symptoms are grouped into three categories: inattention, hyperactivity, impulsivity.

INATTENTION

1. Is easily distracted
2. Doesn't follow directions or finish tasks
3. Doesn't appear to be listening
4. Doesn't pay attention and makes careless mistakes
5. Forgets about daily activities
6. Has problems organizing daily tasks
7. Doesn't like to do things that require sitting still
8. Often loses things
9. Tends to daydream

HYPERACTIVITY

1. Often squirms, fidgets, or bounces when sitting
2. Doesn't stay seated
3. Has trouble playing quietly, is always moving, such as running or climbing on things (In teens and adults, this is more commonly described as restlessness)
4. Talks excessively
5. Is always "on the go" as if "driven by a motor"

IMPULSIVITY

- Has trouble waiting for his or her turn
- Blurts out answers
- Interrupts others

OPPOSITIONAL DEFIANT DISORDER (ODD)

ODD is characterized by a tendency to bother others and exhibit an argumentative and confrontational attitude, aggressiveness towards peers and a disregard for how others feel. ODD sufferers do not respond to reasonable persuasion, regardless of self-interest. Their opposition to all authority figures—especially parents and teachers—is pervasive and constant. It involves a pattern of defiant, angry, antagonistic, hostile, irritable and/or vindictive behaviors. However, it does not necessarily involve violent offenses. Academic failure and poor social adjustment are common complications. Student Noel is an example of such a child.

Individuals with ODD don't choose to act out in this manner. Underlying causes of the disorder are a combination of the child's temperament, biochemical components, environmental issues and perceived neglect. The brain of a person with ODD usually gets stuck, much like a scratched CD repeats the same note over and over again. In addition, depression and tics manifest in people with ODD. (Eric Jensen, 2010) Those with ODD often have difficulty stopping inappropriate behaviors. They become so used to being stuck in a behavior that it becomes more comfortable to fight change than to do what others want them to do. When others continually become annoyed with ODD sufferers, it is easier to develop a combative attitude.

Sufferers typically blame others for their problems. They can be frustrating, tricky, aggressive and deceitful, but in general, they are not dangerous.

CONDUCT DISORDER (CD)

Conduct Disorder is a severe, chronic, pathologically driven and antisocial behavior. It is repetitive and persistent, and it infringes on the basic rights of others and/or violates major societal norms. Students with CD are not the occasional problem learners who disrupt classes; rather, they represent an acute and persistent challenge for teachers. CD is highly correlated with violence and Attention Deficit Disorder (ADD). There are some parallels between Oppositional Defiant Disorder and CD. The single biggest difference between the two is that students with CD will often hurt people, animals and property with zero regard for safety or rules, while students with ODD will not cross these lines.

Students suffering from Conduct Disorder raise personal safety concerns for teachers, other students, family members and/or themselves. Jerry is one student who caused the school and family such concerns.

RECOGNIZABLE SYMPTOMS OF CONDUCT DISORDER

- Inappropriate emotional outbursts with random acts of destruction,

- Consistently hurtful toward peers—swats, hits and verbally intimidates,
- Refuses to follow instructions directly; consistently challenges authority,
- Loud and aggressive communication patterns, often taunting the teacher and using vulgar language,
- Unwilling to participate with others in normal social activities,
- Is prone to lie.

In addition to the conditions outlined above, many students are faced with social factors surrounding their lives over which they have no control. Their family situation is the most pronounced.

SOCIAL FACTORS

As mentioned in the previous chapter, the family but also church and community play an integral part in the socialization of the child. These communities are now extended via social systems online which are limitless. The family as the main agent of socialization still has the greatest impact on the development of the child. In the case of the child with special needs, this dependence on the family is even greater.

Children with conduct disorder may not come from homes where good manners are explicitly practiced. Children who consistently receive negative responses to social and emotional encounters with their primary care-giver(s) learn that other people cannot be relied on, and they ultimately disconnect. In an abusive environment, they learn that the way to get their needs met is to be aggressive and/or violent.

As a result of different socialization experience, members of each gender for the most part develop distinct behavioral expectations, are granted separate opportunities and have different life experiences. The family structure itself is therefore a contributing factor to how individuals behave.

The value which the family places on education is also a contributing factor. If children are from a family background in which emphasis is placed on material things rather than education, then it will be likely that children's values will be misplaced. It is the belief of some teachers that the value of some of these children is reflected in them just wanting to carry the latest cellular phones and being in the latest fashion rather than having the necessary books for school. Hence we see the emphasis on tight pants being altered in keeping with the latest fashion rather than allowing for the following of the school rule which is a necessary part of their education. These students will also be given the latest name-brand bag and shoes, but there are no books in the bag.

Many of these boys also lack male role models or a father figure in the home. Boys are individuals who tend to imitate or model their fathers or male figures at home. They want to watch their fathers do things around the house including seeing him care for his mother. So they see their fathers as role models and try to please them and seek their approval. When these expectations are not addressed, they tend to become antisocial, angry and disruptive in social settings such as school. Boys also need guidance, friendship and approval from their fathers. When a father figure is missing in the home, the boys are twice deprived.

There are cases in which there is a father figure in the home, even the biological father, but the impact is negative rather than positive. Such is the case with student Jason, who lives alone with his father after parental separation. In his case, the separation is accompanied by great hurt, abuse, anxiety and emotional instability in the child, which plays out in disrespectful, angry, disruptive and aggressive behavior..

The presence of instability in the home can be considered a contributing factor to a boy underachieving in school. Instability stems from parents and other family members not getting along with each other. Therefore, the child can feel intense guilt and anger, and portray this kind of behavior at school. Instability can lead to a variety of behavioral problems in children including poor grades, conflicts with other children and bullying, all of which indicate problems at home and a cry for help.

PART 2:
INTERVENTION

CHAPTER 5:
SURE FOUNDATION
EDUCATIONAL CENTRE

The seed for Sure Foundation Educational Centre was sown when I, the CEO/founder, discovered that there was no place in the school system for my son who had been diagnosed with Attention Deficit Hyperactivity Disorder (ADHD) and an associated learning disability. The school which he had been attending simply labelled him as 'bad boy' and treated him as such. I, being a special educator for several years, then made a vow to start a school for children with such needs.

Like my son, many children were being left behind, because they had a disability that was undetected. Children with Attention Deficit Disorder with Hyperactivity form a significant percentage of our school population. This condition is characterized by distractibility, impulsivity and inattentiveness, which usually manifest in what is perceived as poor behavior. It falls in the category of invisible disabilities and is ten times more common in boys than in girls.

These children, along with those with other forms of invisible disabilities, struggle through the system without opportunities to maximize their potentials. Instead, they become a strain on society and, in many cases, resort to crime and violence. Despite the pending danger of leaving these children unattended, the public school system as it exists does not cater to them. Class sizes range from 35 to 45 students, and children with ADHD and other learning difficulties cannot function in them. These children require individual attention and small group settings. Sure Foundation Educational Centre was established to meet the needs of as many of these children as possible within its limited capacity.

Figure 1: Sure Foundation Educational Centre

The school was established as a private non-profit organization for religious and educational purposes only, and registered as a company limited by guarantee without a share capital on December 29, 2004. As a non-profit Christian organization, it would operate under the conviction that every child has the capacity to learn and should be given the opportunity to do so. Against this background, its stated mission was "to provide education for children and young people with learning difficulties in a warm and friendly atmosphere that is conducive to learning, by a trained and motivated staff."

It would seek to carry out this mission through the following processes:

- Providing special education support for students who were currently in school, but who were performing below expected grade level.
- Providing alternative educational opportunities for children and young people who were unable to cope in the regular school system because of learning difficulties.
- Bringing students enrolled in the programme into spiritual awareness of themselves, their potentials, their abilities, and their responsibilities.
- Preparing students to meet qualification specifications to access further educational opportunities.

The school is committed to admitting students who are in need of the service we offer, meeting them at the point of their need, developing programs for them in literacy, numeracy, behavior management, and skills training at moderate costs, thereby lifting their self-esteem and leading them towards the maximization of their God-given potentials. This intervention should result in their being accepted in society as independent, productive and contributing citizens.

Students are admitted to the school following a psycho-educational assessment verifying that they are in need of special education of the kind which the school offers. Guided by this assessment, an Individual Educational Program (IEP) is prepared for each student with objectives in the cognitive and psychosocial domains. The students are then taught individually or in small groups of three to eight, and their progress is measured against their starting points.

While the learning difficulties pose a challenge to teachers, the greater challenge is behavior disorders. For many of these students, Sure Foundation is their last chance for a formal education. The school has put in place a systematic behavior management programme of rewards and consequences supported by a counseling program. However, modification of behavior is a slow process. Coping with inappropriate, violent and aggressive behaviors is an on-going challenge. Yet the school is greatly committed to work with these students to effect behavioral as well as learning changes.

A full-time programme began in September 2006 with the goal of meeting the needs of those students, who were clinically assessed and confirmed with learning disabilities, including those with ADHD who had no alternative school placement. Rejection of such children in school is still prevalent. At the time of writing, the population consists of thirty (30) students assessed with learning disabilities (slow learners, dyslexia, dyscalculia, dysgraphia, poor visual and auditory processing) and behavioral disorders (emotional behavioral disorder, conduct disorder, oppositional defiant disorder, aggression). Eighty percent (80%) of the population are boys. The school is staffed by mature trained teachers with on-going training in special education.

During the life of the school, it has succeeded in moving students from non-readers to grade nine level. There has been increased positive interaction among students, as they move from intrapersonal to interpersonal relationships. They have become more caring and empathetic. Parents and care-givers testify to this. Further, their self-esteem has been lifted as they learn to read, thereby motivating them towards further learning.

In 2009, the school gained registration status with the Ministry of Education, and supervision of the school by the Special Education Unit began. By 2010, we were given a small grant from that Ministry, while they began to access our services to place their children with special needs, paying the prescribed fee for each student that they placed. The Special Education Unit has expressed appreciation for this partnership which has helped to satisfy the nation's need for placements of this special group of students.

In 2011, we began the process of re-integrating students into the mainstream, once they had acquired the requisite reading skills, and since then students have been re-integrated on an annual basis after sitting the grade nine national examination.

The school is working in partnership with the nation's technical vocational training programme for skills training. It is also seeking to establish partnerships with both private and public sectors to accept our students for work experience upon completion of skills training. In addition, partnerships are being sought to provide improved physical space, purchase of equipment to enhance learning, sponsorship of individual students, and facilitation of a school-to-work transition programme.

Students are required to pay moderate fees covering approximately 40% of the real operational cost. These are students from the lower socio-economic stratum of society who are struggling to pay this fee and so cannot be asked to pay more. In addition, several have had to forgo placement, because they cannot afford the fees. Yet, these students need the service offered. Against this background, the school must strive to raise the extra funds to meet operational costs as well as capital expenses.

Several students have passed through the doors of the school since its inception and are now established to various degrees in society, always returning to share their success stories, some of which will be revealed in part three of this book. What follows in the book is mostly based on the operations, experiences and projections of this school with implications for replication of the practices shared therein. The stories cited are all true, confirming the fact that they can make it to success regardless of how they perform when they start the school.

CHAPTER 6:
THE WAY WE WORK—
TEACHING & LEARNING

We begin the process of teaching and learning by creating an environment that is both positive and nurturing. Every day of school begins with worship. Our daily devotion is the most significant part of each day's activity. We recognize that the work with special needs children—especially children with behavior disorders—cannot be done on our own strength. We use the Word of God to instill confidence and self-acceptance in the children. We speak positive words over their lives and encourage them to speak positive things about each other.

Is this easy for them to do? No, but we reinforce our words by prayer, praise and faith, and teach the children to do likewise. We encourage them to memorize Scripture verses such as "I can do all things through Christ who strengthens me." (Philippians 4:13)

In these devotions, individual students are sometimes asked to read the Scriptures, thereby giving them the opportunity to display their reading skills in a meaningful way. Full school devotions are held on

Mondays, class devotions on Tuesdays and Thursdays, gender devotions on Wednesdays, and house devotions on Fridays. The devotions often extend into instructions and discussions in personal development as the need arises. The timetable is sufficiently flexible to make allowance for such occasions.

HOMELY ENVIRONMENT

We seek to establish a homely environment. The small size of the school facilitates this kind of relationship. The school accommodates a maximum of twenty-five students at any one time. Ten members of staff between full-time and part-time serve this population, all of whom assume the roles of "aunts" and "uncles." Students address them as such, and this relationship helps to reinforce a warm and caring environment. Students and teachers are encouraged to treat one another with courtesy and respect.

At the same time, it is a highly-structured environment, one which a theorist may refer to as being restrictive. It is highly recommended that students with special needs are educated in what is described as the least restrictive environment. The least restrictive setting is the general classroom for all students with special accommodation for students with disabilities. For the most restrictive setting, students with disabilities are placed in a separate special education school or institution.

I support this policy of least restrictive environment for children with special needs, excepting where the education of other students is unduly negatively affected by the integration. (Cari Carson, 2015) This position is further supported by Lyndal M. Bullock, expert in Special Education at the University of North Texas. According to him, "The least restrictive environment for a student with EBD might be one that is highly structured, and supportive." (Bullock and Gable, 2006). He continues that "in such an environment, a child with EBD may be able to thrive, learn new behaviors, and make academic progress, whereas, in a less structured setting, a child might not develop socially and academically as would be expected."

In the case of the students at SFEC, many of them had failed to succeed in their least restrictive environment and would continue to fail. Further, as Carson intimates, other students in this general or least restrictive setting could be negatively affected by the integration of children with behavior problems. Against this background, SFEC maintains that its more structured though restrictive setting better serves the needs of these children with behavior challenges. As the students improve in their behavior and learning, they may be re-integrated into the mainstream.

SUCCESS ORIENTATION

Most of our children are of average to above average intelligence, but they struggle in specific areas of learning and behavior. They need to be taught differently and accommodations are made for them where and when necessary. At SFEC, we set out to meet children at the point of their need and strive to give them a sense of success. The school adopts the slogan,

"Success breeds success," and it has witnessed this manifestation, as the students eyes light up at every glimmer of achievement. So we start them from where they are and let them achieve success in baby steps, as the Scripture says, "Precept upon precept, line upon line, line upon line, here a little, and there a little" (Isaiah 28:10).

We seek to structure lessons in a way that keeps them motivated. We do so by adopting strategies that are most likely to bring our students into a sense of achievement and accomplishment. It is against this background that the school has chosen the strategies outlined below as proven effective in the teaching of children with learning disabilities and other special needs. These strategies include individual instruction, differentiated instruction, explicit instruction, scaffolding and the project approach

INDIVIDUAL INSTRUCTION

Individualized instruction focuses on the needs of the individual student. After an assessment to determine a student's present functioning level, specific needs and learning style, an Individualized Educational Programme (IEP) is prepared for that student. This plan most often comprises the subject and content areas where the needs of that student differs from the wider group. At SFEC,

we focus on the core areas of language arts, mathematics and behavior modification.

Learning goals and objectives are established for each child in agreement with that child, and assessment periods for each objective are set. Parents are invited to participate in the final draft of a plan and attach their signatures in agreement. Special times are allocated each week for each student to work on his areas of challenge as defined by the plan.

DIFFERENTIATED INSTRUCTION

Our students are grouped firstly according to their ages and given a class name commensurate to their age group in the regular school system. Our youngest students of 12–14 years are placed in grade 7, which is close to what it would be if they were attending a secondary school. However, the word "special" is added to the number 7—Grade 7special—to avoid confusion about achievement level. While these students are in the same grade based on their ages, they are of different ability and achievement levels and differentiated instruction must be applied as a teaching strategy for each class.

This differentiated instruction includes students who have Individualized Education Programs (IEPs). It doesn't replace the goals and objectives in a child's IEP. Instead the teacher personalizes teaching to help each student meet those goals and objectives. Lesson plans are structured with various objectives for different groups of students. During the delivery of the lessons, questions and activities are directed to each student according to the special objective for him/her. The lesson closes with group activities at the various ability levels.

Flexible groups are at the heart of differentiated instruction. The same students are not in the same group for every activity or assignment. A student may be in one group for mathematics and in a different group for language arts. Likewise, students may be in different groups for activities in keeping with the students individual learning styles and/or capabilities. For example, one group might write a paragraph after discussion around a certain topic, while another group puts on a skit. A third group might create a poster to show what they've learned. Also students in the same class may be reading in groups from different books based on their individual reading levels. At SFEC, differentiated instruction is practiced in most subject areas.

EXPLICIT INSTRUCTION (EI)

Explicit instruction involves using highly structured and sequenced steps to teach a specific skill. It includes 3 components:

1. modeling the skill;
2. providing guided practice with the skill;
3. providing opportunity for independent use of the skill.

At SFEC, this approach is used alongside both individualized and differentiated instruction in the three essential skill areas—reading, writing and mathematics. The instruction follows an 'I do', 'We do', 'You do' model, otherwise defined as modelling, prompting/guided practice and checking or independent practice.

MODELLING (I DO)

This step consists of the teacher demonstrating a task for students and describing exactly what is being done as it is being done. The goal of the modeling step is for the teacher to explicitly state what to do and how to do it. For example, after learning the basic concepts of subtraction and place value of *tens* and *ones*, we may give them the sum:

3 5
-1 8

We tell them, "I will begin with the *ones* column. The bottom number is larger, so I have to take one (1) from the *tens* column. I break that ten into ones. Then I add that ten *ones* to the five *ones* already there. That makes 15 *ones*. Now I take 8 *ones* from the 15 *ones*." We provide several models if necessary.

PROMPTING/GUIDED PRACTICE (WE DO)

This step helps students to gain the confidence and motivation necessary to continue their learning. In this step, we again *tell, ask* and *remind.*

We *tell* them everything they should be doing. We *ask* them questions as we proceed, for example, "What column do we begin with?" "Which number is bigger, the bottom number or the top number?" We proceed in this manner while they carry out the action. We *remind* them of what they should be doing or what questions they should be asking, such as, "Which is bigger?" The teacher leaves them to continue the process, while she walks around and confirms that all students have understood the lesson. The student now has the opportunity to receive feedback while working and on the finished work.

INDEPENDENT PRACTICE (YOU DO)

In this step, the students are allowed to practice with no prompts. Independent practice allows students to put themselves in new learning situations, where they can apply what they have understood from the modeling and guided practice steps. This final learning step provides students with LD an opportunity to test their understanding in order to obtain the highest level of mastery possible with the goal of consolidating their learning. This step also identifies any students who may need some additional support before they move on.

SCAFFOLDING

Scaffolding involves breaking down instructions into smaller, manageable tasks. Students with special needs often have difficulty understanding long-winded or several instructions at once. For children with learning disabilities, it is best to use simple, concrete sentences. We break down a step into a few smaller steps to ensure that our students with special needs understand what we are asking.

At SFEC, we apply the scaffolding approach to seat-work as well as oral instruction. The teacher gives instructions for the work one step at a time, watches the students carry out that step successfully, then moves on to give instruction for the next step. This approach is especially useful for students with EBD in addition to learning disability, as this forces them to attend to the teacher constantly in order to complete a task. It increases the time on task but decreases levels of disruptive behavior by students.

PROJECT APPROACH

The Project Approach is an educational model that enables teachers to guide students through in-depth studies of real world topics. At SFEC, we witness the motivation of students as they become actively involved in their own learning. The students then produce higher quality work and grow as individuals and collaborators.

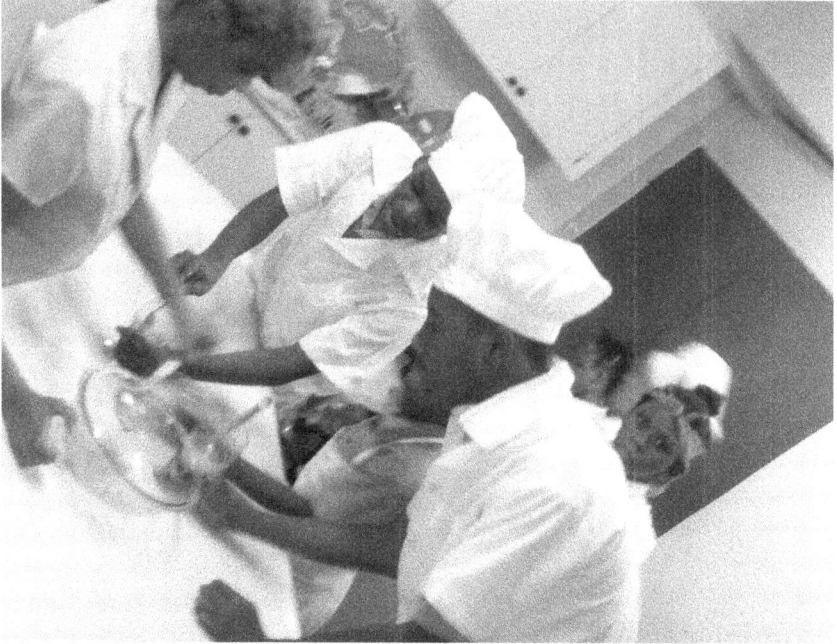

The beliefs upon which the Project Approach rests are as follows:

1. All children come to school with a quest to understand their experiences; all children want to learn.
2. School is life, and teachers and students should experience their time in school as real life rather than seeing these two as separated and unrelated spheres.
3. Students construct their own knowledge but also need teachers to facilitate and guide this process.
4. Students have diverse strengths, weaknesses, interests and backgrounds; capitalizing on

these differences enables students to learn from each other and to grow as individuals.

5. Students learn best when they have a positive self-esteem and sense of purpose.
6. Students learn through a mixture of first-hand observation, hands-on experience, systematic instruction and personal reflection.
7. Teaching and learning are interactive processes.
8. Social and emotional skills are as important as academic skills and knowledge.
9. Classrooms are flexible learning spaces that support and adapt to student needs. (The Project Approach, 2015).

All of these factors are good reasons why we consider this approach as an effective tool for harnessing the energy, interest and learning opportunities of the student with LD and EBD. Therefore, at SFEC, we have put this approach to the test and find it effective in achieving curricular goals.

Other strategies and creative approaches are introduced from time to time as necessary and at the imagination of individual teachers. However, those mentioned in this chapter are the ones that undergird the operation of the school.

CHAPTER 7:
THE WAY WE WORK—
BEHAVIOR MANAGEMENT

The work of the school begins with the establishment of an environment that is warm, friendly and homely. Almost all students attending the school come with behavior challenges of one kind or the other. That's the main reason they come to us. They have been accustomed to hearing about their bad behavior again and again in school situations, at home and in the community. The school operates on the understanding that we cannot control the behavior choices of anyone else, no matter how many threats or criticisms we throw at each other. If we can't control others, then all we can do is encourage one another and support one another in the goals we have. Therefore, the school takes the position of bringing the students into conformity through a process of encouragement while ensuring that learning takes place.

Their social maladjustments manifest in various kinds of behavior and require individual behavioral treatment. Therefore, the school must cater to individual needs while at the same time establishing structures and systems that are applicable to the whole school. We do this by preparing individual behavior programmes (IBP) as well as a school-wide behavior management system.

The school-wide behavior management programme does more than monitoring behavior. Driven by the conviction that success breeds success, the behavior programme is meant to reinforce both learning and behavior through a system of rewards and consequences. It is an award system for all forms of learning and effort. It provides immediate reinforcement for accomplishments, is consistent with rules and discipline, corrects errors and rewards students when they make these corrections themselves. It explains behavioral expectations, and it teaches and demonstrates appropriate behaviors rather than just expecting these students with special needs to pickup such on their own.

SYSTEM OF AWARDS

The school's award system is patterned after the token economy framework. Points are awarded according to table below:

Completion of homework	Completion of class work	Following the rules	Interpersonal Relationships	Total
1	2	3	4	10

Table 7.1 – Daily Point system

INTERPERSONAL RELATIONSHIP

As you have noticed above, interpersonal relationships is most heavily weighted, because this is the area of greatest challenge for these students with EBD. It includes relationship with both staff and students demonstrated by their respect for teachers and treatment of each other. Unfortunately, the behavior problems of children with ADHD often affect their relationships not just with adults but with other children as well, as clinical psychologist David Anderson points out. He is director of the ADHD and Behavior Disorders Center at the Child Mind Institute, Southern California, and attests to the fact that there are a host of reasons why we see friendships being impaired by ADHD symptoms.

He explains that for children who are highly distractible, it could be that they can't keep up with a pace of conversation, and their friends just notice they're zoned out. For the child who's really impulsive, it may be that they interrupt other children and don't let anybody else get a word in edgewise. For children who have real difficulty delaying gratification, it may be that they always have to choose the activity, and anybody who doesn't want to go along with this gets impulsive speech directed at them, sometimes leading to explosive and retaliatory behavior patterns.

During the day, the teacher documents evidences of aggressive behavior, retaliation or vindictive behavior, defiance, offence to other students and/or use of obscene language. These behaviors are recorded by a check list which forms a part of the comments on the Student's Daily Record.

COMMENTS					
Loses Temper	Defies Adults	Annoys Others	Vindictive Behavior	Obscene Language	Other

Table 7.2: Behavior Checklist

The full Daily Record Sheet is presented in Appendix A. At the end of the day, points are subtracted from the student's total score accordingly.

FOLLOWING THE RULES

The general school rules are agreed upon by parents and students evidenced by their signatures of agreement, copies of which are placed in the students' files for reference. These rules were established collaboratively by past students, teachers and parents, and then ratified by the Board and are non-negotiable for a set period such as the year. Rules are publicly displayed in the school and discussed periodically at general assembly and the class level.

In addition, there are specific class rules governing the conduct of classes. These rules are established by each class with input and agreement from both teacher and students. Some of these rules, once established are also non-negotiable such as:

1. Be punctual for session.
2. Gather your tools for work at the beginning of each session.
3. Raise your hand to ask or answer a question.

Other rules may be negotiable, such as "Eat your lunch in your classroom" and "Lunch break will be forty minutes only." Students lose one point for each rule broken and could end up with a negative score in that column. However, this rarely happens.

COMPLETING WORK

While correctness of work done is important, students are not penalized for incorrect work. Instead, they are rewarded for completing the work given. What is to be enforced are (1) effort and (2) discipline to complete tasks. Students are given differentiated activities, so no child is given work which is above his/her capability.

Individual assistance is given to the student who is challenged in any special way. More time is spent with that student in guided assistance before proceeding to independent work. For example, in the case of mathematics, the teacher may do three problems with a student before giving him/her one to do independently. After the student completes one or two correctly, then he/she is given a few as a class activity. He then earns his points upon completion of those sums given.

HOMEWORK

Homework is assigned to students on a daily basis consistent with the awarding of points. The purposes of developing discipline towards work is to help children review and practice what they have learnt and to develop their research skills. This gives parents the opportunity to be involved in the educational process of their children in a meaningful way.

Parents are required to sign their children's homework as evidence that they have seen the homework. In this way, parents are indirectly forced to encourage the completion of the homework. They are also expected to give assistance where necessary and possible, especially in the area of research.

Daily Record

The points for each day are agreed upon in a class evaluation session at the end of each day and recorded on a Daily Record Sheet. Every student is involved in peer evaluation in conjunction with the teacher, and this time is often a heated one, because every point is important to each student. This process is an important part of the school's daily routine and is systematically carried out by all teachers and students.

Aggregated Points System

The points are aggregated at the end of each month, and students are rewarded according to the percentage of possible points that they acquire. Absences from school automatically results in deprivation of possible points. The names of students with the top five scores of eighty percent (80%) and above are posted publicly for the viewing of the school population and visitors to the school. The student with the highest score is acclaimed 'Student of the Month' and his/her photograph posted. Students who earn eighty percent and above for three consecutive months earn a 'Merit Award' badge. Students who earn eighty percent and above for six consecutive months earn an 'Honour Student' badge.

At the end of a semester, each student's point standing is transferred to merit points at twenty-five points per merit and recorded on their progress report. Students are further awarded in more tangible ways at the end of the school year, and from their accumulated point standing for the year, a student of the year is recognized.

ACCOMMODATIONS

Accommodations are made for students with ADHD and Autism. The students with autistic tendencies are usually rigid in their behaviors and insistent in doing what they choose. Once these fixations are determined, the teacher seeks the cooperation of the rest of the class to allow them the privileges. For example, Renaldo has a fixed seat and that is the only seat he will sit in; whatever re-organization of seating is required, he is allowed to move with his desk and chair.

Students with ADHD are allowed physical activity breaks, such as standing, stretching and moving around the room. Efforts are made to teach the more academic subjects in the morning at the group or individual level. In addition, they are given tasks to do where possible such as running errands around the school or organizing the classroom. Students who work fast are given the opportunity to choose a pleasant activity to occupy themselves while waiting on others to complete their task.

Students with dysgraphia are allowed to do their writing on the computer. Provisions may be made for them to be provided with laptops for use on a consistent basis.

SYSTEM OF CONSEQUENCES

With our best efforts at motivating students and awarding them accordingly, some will and have failed along the way. Therefore aligned to the school rules are consequences for deviation from them. There is an established procedure for dealing with such deviations including persistent disruptive behaviors. These consequences are applied following the steps below:

1. Loss of Points

The school rules clearly state the circumstances under which points are lost.

2. Time Out from Class

Students are given time-out when their behaviors become disruptive, thereby interfering with the learning process of other students. These are short breaks away from the class during which time students are expected to reflect on their conduct in a repentant manner. When invited back to class, often they are required to apologize for their behavior.

3. In School Counselling

Students are referred to the office if they persistently break the rules of the class, or become disrespectful to their teacher at any time. They are counselled, warned, and sometimes logged depending on the magnitude of the offence. Once students are logged, points are deducted from their scores at the end of that month. The student may also be referred to other counsellors within the school.

4. In School Disciplinary Action

We invite students to suggest ways that they should be disciplined in the event of blatant disobedience or repeated breaking of the rules. Some of the suggestions they give are followed. Of these, the ones that the school often apply are writing of lines, public apology or standing in a corner.

5. Parental Intervention

Parents are requested to come in for discussion about their children's behavior in the case of any serious offence, where the student blatantly refuses to accept the disciplinary action meted out by the school or for persistent or repeated offences. Upon parents' responses, conferences are held with the child, parent, another member of staff, the counsellor, and the principal. The child's life and conduct both at home and school are discussed, and decisions and commitments are made by each participant. Invariable, the child's offensive behavior stems from circumstances within the family setting.

6. Referral for Professional Counselling

Based on the outcome of the parental conference and/or recurring like behaviors, a child may be referred for professional counselling at the Child Guidance clinic or to a private psychologist or psychiatrist. In the case of any outbursts of uncontrolled rage, that child may also be referred to the police community service for additional counselling.

7. Signing of Behavior Contract

If after successive counselling sessions and monitoring, there is no evidence of effort towards change by that student, then he/she is required to sign a behavior contract. The contract is an agreement to comply with certain codes of conduct or accept the related consequences which could include deprivation of time at school.

8. Time Out at Home

In the case of repeated disruptive behavior persisting after most or all fore-going measures have been applied, the student may be given time-out from school for no more than one day.

9. Suspension

Suspension from school is a last resort prior to the Board's intervention. A student may be suspended for any one grave offence as outlined in the school rules. These include fighting. In addition, a student who is persistently disruptive after going through all processes outlined above may be suspended.

10. School Board Intervention

A student may be referred to the Board after repeated suspensions or for any one grave offence such as the use of a weapon or threat to life.

11. Part-time Arrangement

The school is hesitant to exclude students, because many of them have already had their full share of exclusions. The Board may agree to give the offending student an opportunity to continue school on a part time basis on designated days per week, if he/she threatens the smooth operation of the school after some or all previous processes have been applied. The school maintains its relationship with the child during the out days by way of assignments to be completed. During this time, if there is evidence of improved effort by the student as reflected in his/her daily record, then he/she may be reintegrated into the full-time programme.

12. Parental Withdrawal

If the student fails to conform after going through all phases up to number eleven, then the School Board has no option but to ask his/her parent to withdraw him/her. Of the over one hundred students treated by the school up to the time of this writing, there was only one such case.

PART 3:
IMPACT

Students' image of the school as a hospital for children with special needs.

Parents' image of the school as a nurturing mother caring for children, no matter what are their differences and leading them to brighter days.

CHAPTER 8:
AN APPRECIATIVE INQUIRY

Meeting our children at the point of their need and developing programs to move them forward is a reasonable thing to do, but how can one truly tell that progress has been made or that the program is effective? I sought to answer these questions in my doctoral research under the title "A Vision and Plan for the Growth of the Sure Foundation Educational Centre: A Model for Special Education as a Means For The National Transformation of Jamaica." (Ricketts, 2016). In this research, I sought feedback from the main stakeholders in the school—students, parents, teachers, and Board members—through the process of an Appreciative Inquiry (AI).

The research was carried out in 2015. This form of research was first introduced by David Cooperrider and his associates at case Western Reserve University in the mid-eighties. It is governed by a number of assumptions and is carried out in a five phase process described as the 5-D Cycle. The basic assumption of the AI is that in every organization something works and that change can be managed by identifying what works and then analyzing how to do more of what works. It suggests that we appreciate what works in an organization rather than focusing on the problem. Instead of analyzing problems, you analyze success. (Cooperrider, 2005, Hammond 1998).

THE 5-D CYCLE

Define

The first D is to define what we are going to inquire about. Here we decide on the topic we want to investigate. You do this by looking for what gives life to the organization and by questioning people about what they value about themselves, their work and the organization. Through this process, a topic for investigation is agreed upon. In our case, the topic which we agreed upon was "Bringing Out the Best in Our Children." We wanted to know how well we were succeeding in bringing out the best in these children with learning and behavior challenges.

Discover

The next D is the discovery phase. In this phase, you seek to discover the best of what presently exists. You look at the organization with an "appreciative eye." Questions are formulated about personal values, experiences and hopes for the organization, and interviews conducted in pairs accordingly.

Dream

The third D represents the Dream Phase. In this phase, the information from the interviews is presented to a wider group in order to discover common themes. With these themes, the group can now dream of what the future might look like.

Design

The fourth D stands for Design. This is the decision-making phase. Here you write directions to achieve the future that the group has decided upon. These take the form of provocative propositions which state each decision in the present tense as if it was already achieved. For example, "We are a school that meets the needs of all our children regardless of the challenges and disorders they come with." According to Hammond, "the purpose of provocative propositions is to keep our best at a conscious level as we work to deliver what we envisioned" (Hammond, loc. 374).

Deliver

The fifth and final phase is Deliver/Destiny. This phase is to deliver by putting systems in place to create the future which the group envisioned. The provocative propositions may now lead to policy or system changes in order to meet desired goals.

I believed that the positive nature of this approach to research could not only give me feedback on the impact of the school program, but also lead to necessary changes. Against this background we embarked on the following 5-D process.

RESEARCH PROCESS

The first phase of the research was undertaken by the teaching staff, who agreed on the topic "Bringing Out the Best in our Children." Participants of the second and third phases—Discover and Dream—were past and present students, past and present parents, teaching staff, supporting staff and members of the Board. The fourth phase, Design, was carried out by a core group of teachers, while the final phase, Deliver, is still in process and is being led by management and staff. Data was collected through a number of questions posed in interviews with individual persons during the discovery session (See Appendix B).

All participants were fully cooperative in the research process, vibrant, enthusiastic and seemed to be enjoying themselves. They actually appreciated the opportunity to express their opinions in this non-threatening evaluative exercise.

The students' level of understanding and appreciation despite their disabilities was a pleasant and surprising factor to me. For example, during the Discovery phase, in answer to the question "What do you value most in life?", the major values identified among them were family, education, friendships, relationship with God, technology, material things, life and peace in Jamaica. These responses indicated sound and higher order thinking above my own expectations, given what appeared to be their thoughtless behaviors. In answer to the question "What do you like best about the school?", they lauded the teachers, the small classes, the individual attention, the real life experiences, the skills training and the award system. While expressing appreciation, they also acknowledged that there were other things to be desired. They demonstrated that they could critically evaluate the school.

POSITIVE CORE OF THE SCHOOL

During the discovery phase of the research, a number of factors surfaced repeatedly, an indication that these were the factors that were giving life to the school. These were elements of appreciation and value placed on the services of the school and together, they constitute the positive core of the school. Here are the most outstanding ones based on the frequency of occurrence:

1. small classes and individual attention given to students
2. encouragement, love, and care of the teachers
3. love, empathy, and sincerity of the students
4. family-type relationship
5. award system to support discipline and performance
6. Christian values taught and upheld
7. students' willingness to accept their mistakes and make corrections
8. skills training the students receive
9. experience trips and real life examples that are brought to bear on learning
10. opportunities for teachers to learn about children with special needs

These factors also reveal the ethos of the school. The students liked the fact that there were not a lot of children in the class, so they could get one-to-one attention. A number of students had commendations for the school's teaching of godly things, encouragement to the students, regular communication with the students and maintaining a peaceful environment. Most significant was their recommendation for the continuation of the school to provide opportunities for students like themselves. This sentiment was brought out clearly in the testimony of past student Alrick, who had then moved on to higher learning but continued to ascribe his success to the help he received at SFEC. He had this to say:

Sure Foundation Educational Centre is a small school with a lot of potential. I remember when I first came to this institution. To tell you the truth, I hated this school. The teachers showed me love, and all I showed them was anger and hate. I tried countless times to leave this school, but no matter how I tried, I could not leave. I began to misbehave, hoping they would then kick me from this school, but it just got worse. The more I gave them trouble, the more they loved me.

The only way I could get out of this school was to complete the GNAT [Grade Nine Achievement Test]. That was my only chance for freedom, but that would come at a cost. I had to work hard and study, but how could I study when I couldn't even read? I can remember the teachers telling me to settle down and behave myself. Well, eventually, I settled down. Then I began to read better and even became the Student of the Month at the school. Now look where I am. I am a prefect at the St. Andrew Technical High School. I am also a student counsellor and a cadet. If it was not for this school, I would be nowhere. I would be lost.

I am grateful for what this school has done for me. My only wish is that this school be recognized as the best private school in Jamaica for children with special needs.

The appreciation of parents and teachers was also evident. By their responses, what teachers valued most about the school was the opportunity it provided them to learn about children with special needs, and that learning has affected them to become more empathetic and tolerant towards these children. They also valued the small size of the school which helped to facilitate a sense of family. The projection of Christian values reinforced by a system of discipline was also included as being valued by them.

The parents' greatest appreciation of the school was the individual attention received by their children, followed by the encouragement, love and care that they and their children received. The small classes and the progress of their children seemed to go hand in hand. One parent expressed her appreciation in this way:

When my child came to this school at age 13, he could do nothing. This school took him off the ground and gave both he and myself hope. It gives me a reason to go on. I never knew that he could learn.

While acknowledging the positive things about the school, the research also brought to light a number of the factors that militate against the school operating at optimum efficiency.

PREFERRED FUTURE

Some negative factors surfaced during the *Discovery* session and were further emphasized during the *Dream* session. The most outstanding of these factors were:

1. inadequate building facilities to accommodate the required skills training;
2. lack of play and a recreational area;
3. insufficient classroom resources to enhance program delivery;
4. insufficient specialist practitioners in essential areas;
5. inadequate financial resources for basic programs;
6. and insufficient parental support.

Both the positive core and the needs of the school were incorporated in dreams for the preferred future of the school.

Responses to questions posed on the future of the school indicated that the participants had a clear vision of their preferred future, and that future was one built on that which already existed. All participants expressed the desire to move the school toward greater levels of success. In answer to the question "What would you like your school to look like for the future?", nearly all students expressed the desire for (1) a change of location to one with a playfield and (2) upgraded facilities to accommodate more students and (3) an expanded program. Some current students desired greater publicity to inform the public of the existence of the school and attract more students.

In an interview with a sample of parents, the first question asked them directly was: "How satisfied are you with your child's progress in this school?" Listed responses ranged from 'very satisfied' to 'very dissatisfied.' Sixty percent selected 'satisfied.' The other forty percent selected 'partially satisfied.' They gave comments such as "satisfied to about 75 percent," "satisfied to a degree, but not fully," "he has shown progress, but not enough," and "satisfied with teachers' efforts, but not certain if the teachers have full understanding of working with special children." These comments point to the fact that, while not totally dissatisfied, parents' expectations were greater than what they were seeing.

During the *Dream* session, both children and adults were asked to draw images that could best illustrate what they envisioned the school to look like when at its best. The children all agreed that the drawing of a hospital by a sixteen-year-old boy was their best illustration of what the school would look like at its best. The following narrative was written as a provocative proposition, as if that desire was already fulfilled:

My school is like a hospital. The children who come here have special needs. The hospital attends to their needs, and helps them to learn well. It is a caring environment.

The image selected by the adults was one portraying the school as a mother with her children as produced by a parent. The narrative read:

> When we are at our best, we are like a nurturing mother—caring for children no matter what are their differences—leading them to brighter days.

The provocative propositions made during the *Dream* phase were further refined and expanded during the *Design* phase (see Appendix C). It culminated in a vision for the school as follows:

> As an established Christian NGO, fully accountable for its operations, Sure Foundation Educational Centre is a school that equips its students to move on to institutions of higher learning and/or take their place in society as independent productive citizens in jobs suitable to their skills and capabilities. Programs are designed to meet the special needs of all our students and are carried out at the individual level in a warm and friendly environment with qualified, encouraging, and motivating staff. Our students develop self-esteem, perseverance, self-control, respect, and responsibility, while taking active part in decision making. Our programs are maintained by adequate support from parents and other partners in education.

The final phase of the AI process, *Delivery/Destiny*, began with the implementation of innovative classroom strategies. These include the Project Approach, Scaffolding Seatwork, and an upgrading of the Token

Economy System of Behavior Management, all of which were outlined in Chapters 6 and 7. These strategies have had a positive effect on bringing the best out of our children. However, full realization of this vision will involve reinforced concentration on areas of strength identified such as school climate, and concerted efforts towards areas of weakness such as parental support and the nurturing of partners to ensure financial viability.

CHAPTER 9:
STUDENT OUTCOME

Many persons with disabilities have excelled and taken up their places of responsibilities in society. Like Paul, they have accepted their condition, and use it as a source of motivation to draw out their full potentials with the help of God (2 Cor. 11:30; 2 Cor. 7:4b; 2 Cor. 13:4b; Rom. 5:3). This includes my own son who put his ADHD and learning disabilities in proper perspective and forged ahead to complete an associate degree, and at the time of writing, now holds one full-time job as clerical assistant/systems administrator in a school while also completing his first degree in Information Technology.

The students of SFEC experience weaknesses in mental acuity, emotional unrest, in some cases rejection by parents and society, a sense of failure, disappointments and absence of love. Yet, with help of their teachers and some support from parents, they have striven for excellence in accordance with the school's motto: "Reaching Upwards; Striving for Excellence." I often tell people that what the school seeks to do is to "bathe them in love, and dry them with grace." Though firm with them, teachers never treat them as they may deserve based on the world's standards. That level of acceptance has set the stage for drawing the best out of them. Neither do we judge their success against the standards of others but rather against their own potentialities.

One Jamaican saying is "The test of the pudding is in the eating." Since the goal of the school is "To prepare students for independent productive citizens," then we must examine the evidence of such outcome. It is with this intention that SFEC has sought to follow its students beyond school, and record the adjustments they have made into the real world and their contribution to society. There are three exit/transition pathways from the school. In this chapter we look at our students achievements by these pathways.

Continuing Education

Reintegration

The first option is for students to reintegrate into the mainstream at age fifteen after having sat the Grade Nine Achievement Test (GNAT). Students may sit this examination at any time that they show readiness within the age limit of fourteen to fifteen years.

Noel and Jason are two such students. You will recall that both came to SFEC after being excluded from at least three schools because of behavior problems. Both students went through the behavior management programme including the consequences of partial attendance. Noel eventually earned his way back into full-time attendance having made significant progress in less than one year after attending SFEC. He learnt to discipline himself, expressed appreciation for the caring environment of the school and focused on his academic learning enough to earn high grades in the GNAT examination, thereby receiving placement in the school of his first choice. Jason's progress in behavior change was less outstanding, but he maintained himself enough to complete the GNAT examination and was reintegrated into the mainstream.

We read about Alrick in Chapter 8, where he gave his story of his sojourn at SFEC and how it prepared him for great success at the St. Andrew Technical High School. He went on to achieve several awards in academic achievements and leadership roles, passed five subjects at the Caribbean Examinations Council (CXC) achieving the Caribbean Secondary Education Certificate (CSEC), two subjects in City and Guilds examinations, and four subjects at the National Council on Technical and Vocational Education and Training (NC-TVET) examinations. He was then admitted to the twelfth and thirteenth grades for advanced studies and succeeded in six subjects in the Caribbean Advanced Proficiency Examination (CAPE). At the time of writing, he is pursuing his college education for a career in Business Administration. Four years after leaving the school, he returned as motivational speaker at the school's graduation exercise.

SKILLS TRAINING

Students who have reached the age of sixteen and did not qualify for the GNAT are then prepared for skills training through the nation's vocational training programme, the Human Employment and Resource Training (HEART) Trust/ National training Agency (NTA) which focusses primarily on competency. Through this programme, they may obtain certification by way of the National Vocational Qualification of Jamaica (NVQ-J) at levels 1–5. These are certificates of competence are given to HEART Trust/NTA trainees and other industry workers after a series of performance based assessments. They are certified as proof that they have the skills, knowledge and understanding to perform in accordance to workplace requirements. The NVQ-J's are granted by the NCTVET, which is the island's only certification body for technical and vocational skills training.

Special provision is made for young people with disabilities through the Abilities Foundation of Jamaica. Here, they are exempted from the regular entrance examination and accommodated with extended time to complete the required training programme. Therefore, the Abilities Foundation is SFEC's first choice of referral for technical/ vocational training for our students moving forward.

Norado Rhoden and Dane Fearon are among those students who followed this route. Dane successfully completed a two-year programme in Woodwork qualifying him for the NVQ-J, level 1 in Carpentry. He is now gainfully employed at one of the nation's leading firms in the business. Norado also successfully completed his two-year programme qualifying him for NVQ-J level 1 in Business and went on to work experience at a government agency, where he then gained full-time employment.

Other students have sat the general entrance examination for the HEART trust/NTA institutions and succeeded in completing the first and second training levels in the same time as non-disabled students. Rusean Allen is one such student. He applied for the academy during his final year at SFEC, passed the entrance examination, pursued the course in electrical installation and graduated with a level two certificate after three years. He gained employment in the country's leading power industry immediately upon graduation.

SCHOOL TO WORK TRANSITION

There are some students whose social adjustment as well as their academic functioning makes it impossible for them to integrate at any other training programme, even after years in our programme. However, they must be prepared for independent living. The option for them after the age of seventeen is to introduce them to skill training through a school-to-work transition programme. They are engaged as observers at a workplace willing to facilitate them for specific times each week. By this process, they gradually gain hands-on experience on specified days and attend school on the other days. The school maintains an on-going relationship with the workplace for monitoring the students' participation and conduct. Those days out are still recorded as school days which must be accounted for.

Such a relationship is maintained between school and workplace while the student gradually increases time at the place of work, until he/she is fully integrated socially and vocationally. At this time, a request is made for the student to be fully engaged at the workplace as an apprentice. At the time of writing, Abigail and Jordon are two students moving on to this programme. This is the final phase of the school programme as we seek to ensure that all students successfully transition to the next level.

ON THE JOB

Research has shown that employers are generally satisfied with work-related performance of persons with disabilities. Words such as "honest," "well-motivated" and "reliable" have been used to describe persons with mild intellectual disabilities. However, they differ in the level of social support they need in order to reach high levels of performance.

I spoke with some of the employers of our past students, and the feedback I received was mostly positive. Past students were satisfying employers' expectations and described as doing well—holding their jobs, willing, helpful, ready to take instructions, punctual, motivated, reliable, and dependable. However, there were limitations in handling complex problems.

It is true also that the employers differed in their degree of tolerance for the workers' limitations. For best results, the employers need coaching on the possible challenges of each worker with a disability, especially the invisible disabilities such as learning disability and ADHD. The employer can then make a reasoned decision whether or not they are prepared to work with such a person and make necessary accommodations for him/her, such as steering them away from functions which demand much intricate skills; for example, mathematical configurations if this is an area of weakness.

The past students of SFEC have shown that they can achieve academically, vocationally and socially, and make the necessary adjustments to fit into adult life as independent contributing citizens. This achievement is not without the help of loving, caring and accommodating persons around them, even to the workplace according to their individual needs. It cannot be a case of one size fits all. They differ in needs and circumstances, and their special needs accompany them into adulthood.

PART 4:
PARTNERSHIP

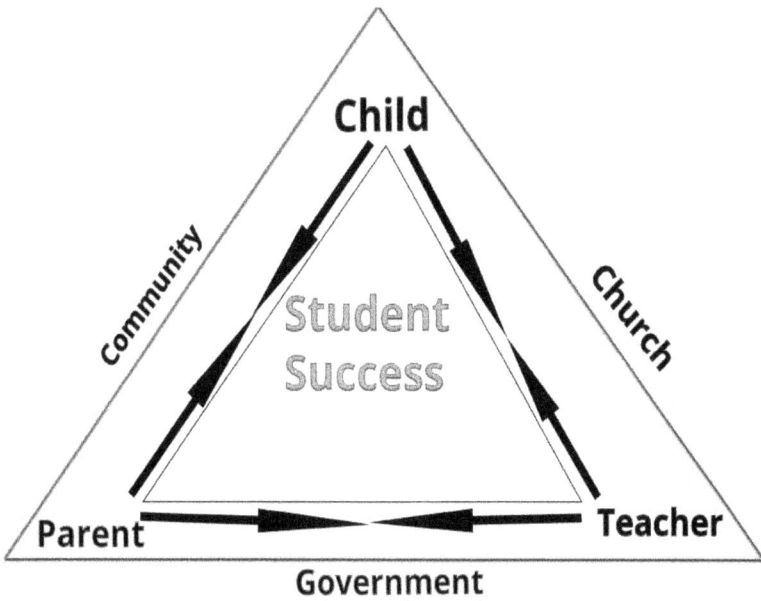

CHAPTER 10:
THE PLACE OF PARENTS

I know what it means to be the parent of a child with special needs. Richard came to me at the age of two years. I soon recognized that he was running all over the place, not listening to me, insistent on following his own path and about to drive me crazy. By the time he was four years old, I knew that I could not manage this child on my own.

I sought a referral from my general practitioner to the Child Guidance Clinic. It was the help of the Child Guidance Clinic at the Bustamante Hospital for Children with Dr. Judith Lieba, and consistent behavior management strategies at home, that I successfully raised that child through childhood and adolescence. At SFEC, I offer the same strategies to other parents, because I have the evidence that these can work.

Nonetheless, I know that it may not be as easy for other parents to follow my example, because I operated from the vantage point of an educator. I was an educator for children with special needs both at home and at school. Few parents have this privilege. Their circumstances are very different, yet they are required and expected to raise their children with special needs to the best of their ability. Where do they begin, and how should they proceed? I hope to provide some answers to these questions.

COPING STYLE

I fully understand that being the parent of any child with a disability is a stressful situation. Parents go through various stages of emotional responses including denial and rejection. Meanwhile, the child goes through his own struggles. Children with learning disabilities and Attention Deficit Hyperactive Disorder (ADHD) are usually very disorganized. They have trouble dealing with sequences and order, so they don't plan well. They are easily distracted and often impulsive. Children with any form of behavior disorder are constant irritants to the family. They tend to leave everyone on edge, because their behavior is often unpredictable, erratic and inconsistent.

Parents are required to learn coping strategies for themselves as well as develop strategies for helping their children to overcome their struggles effectively. That's a tall order but absolutely necessary. Michal Al-Yagon is an Associate Professor at Tel Aviv University and researcher in School Counselling and Special Education. In an article "Socioemotional and Behavioral Adjustment Among School-Age Children With Learning Disabilities," he examined the role of a mother's attachment style, coping strategies, effect on the socioemotional and behavior adjustment and secure attachment of school age children with Learning Disability (LD). The study showed that mothers of children with

LD reported lower levels of active coping,and higher levels of depression in comparison to mothers of children without LD. Meanwhile, their children with LD reported higher loneliness, lower sense of coherence, lower goal directed energy, lower planning to meet goals and less attachment security compared to their typically developing peers. According to the writer, the results demonstrated that when the mother showed higher use of avoidant coping, the association between her child's disabilities and feelings of loneliness became stronger. (Al-Yagon, 2005).

I believe that many of our children including some of those identified in this book are victims of parents who shy away from coping with their behaviors, and who are hoping that the school will provide the necessary solutions both for themselves and their children. This is so because, to a large extent, they do not know how to cope. Parent training is essential and must form a part of any programme for children with special needs. At SFEC, training seminars form a regular part of the programme, and we think of creative ways to get our parents out for such training. As motivation, we have built the attendance into a parent contract and included it as a part of parental rating for annual awards.

PARENT CHILD RELATIONSHIP

Having good relationships and setting appropriate limits with children is important at all developmental stages, and it's especially important for the child with special needs. The parents must be mindful of the child's struggle as well as their struggle as parents.

One way to build a positive relationship with the child is to practice simply being present with him without trying to change anything about him. Children appreciate this quality time more than anything else. While writing this book, I asked my son, now grown and doing well, "Son, what stands out most for you in my parenting that I could share with other parents?" He answered, "Being there for me, taking time to listen to me, even in your busiest times, taking time to teach me, keeping school with me, being interested in me. Not just having me as a son but being interested in me."

In addition to their own relationship with the child, parents must teach their children how to relate to other persons in a positive and respectful manner. Children with learning disabilities often have problems with relationships.

"They don't read social signals: facial expressions, gestures, or tones of voice very well. Additionally, many of these children are literal and concrete; they cannot deal with subtleties, nuances, inferences, or multiple meanings." (Smith, 2002)

They need to be taught explicitly how to relate to others beginning in the family with siblings and other adults. Parents have to work with them on reading faces, gestures and movements, and on learning what is and is not appropriate to say (Smith, 2002). At school, students often say things that are quite inappropriate for relating to each other, their teachers or any adult. Yet they cannot see any errors in their communication. "Parents may have to coach them through common social situations until they develop appropriate interpersonal behaviors" (Smith, 2002).

Most importantly, love must undergird all efforts towards a positive parent-child relationship. At the heart of relationship is emotion. The parent's feelings about the child and the child's perception of how his parent feels about him will definitely impact the relationship . Andrew, mentioned in Chapter 2, believes that his parents' love is skewed towards his brother and not himself; this perception has a devastating effect on him both at home and at school, reflecting in poor social behavior and academic achievement. Parents must reflect, recognize and own up to their feelings about the children, as well as their own frustrations and disappointments which come to bear on their patience and attitude towards their children with special needs. Is their attitude one of unconditional love? If that is the case, it will influence their behavior towards their children. The children will sense this. They will know that their parents are there for them irrespective of how they behave. They do not have to behave to win the love of their parents. They will want to behave, because they love their parents and want to be obedient. When a love relationship is firmly established between child and parent, behavior management becomes more effective.

BEHAVIOR MANAGEMENT

Research reveals that behavioral problems occur most often in families when parents do these three things:

1. Fail to notice when children behave well.
2. Pay too much attention to negative behavior.
3. Make empty threats or escalating demands on children.

Most parents spend more time addressing bad behavior and pay less or no attention to good behavior. Yet even when a child is at his worst, he still does things that are good some of the times. Research has shown that when behaviors are attended to or nurtured, they grow stronger and occur more frequently. Behaviors that are unnoticed may weaken or disappear. Parents should think about what their children do that they would like them to do more frequently or consistently and let the children know exactly what they did well. If you are a parent, you will notice how your child's countenance lights up with glee. He will want to do the same thing again, just to hear those words of praise. A little praise goes a long way.

REINFORCEMENT AT HOME

Reinforcement of good behavior can be very effective when practiced at home. Giving your child positive reinforcement for being good helps maintain ongoing good behavior. Positive attention enhances the quality of the relationship, improves self-esteem and feels good for everyone involved. This is the approach that I used with my own child with LD and ADHD systematically for most of his childhood years with rewards and consequences agreed upon by child and parent. Rewards are most effective as motivators when the child can choose from a variety of things: extra time on the iPad, a special treat, etc.

Positive attention to brave behavior can also help attenuate anxiety; this helps kids become more receptive to instructions and limit-setting. This attention is especially important to children with any form of behavior disorder. Rewards should be linked to specific behaviors and always delivered consistently. At home, I kept a book in which I recorded the behaviors and both the rewards and the consequences attached to each, which represented a contract. That written contract helped me to be consistent, because my child himself would ensure this.

Referring to my son again, he testifies to the benefits of the reward system. While writing this book, I asked him what he valued most about my system of behavior management.

The reward system is what I liked most. It motivated me and helped me to behave myself better. The fact that I would get a reward at the end of my efforts made me want to try. I tried to do less walking up and down because I would get more points, and more points meant a better reward.. The reward system worked for me. It was a good motivator both for work and behavior. The fact that my teacher had to record my behavior and report to my mother made me behave better at school. I liked it that I had a say in the choice of my reward. I was also motivated by the knowledge that the type of grades that I got on my school report would help to determine the quantity and quality of my rewards.

HOME/SCHOOL RELATIONSHIP

Parents are integral partners in the education of their children. The child comes to school fortified with his experiences from home. He does not leave the home-related factors at home. Rather, he brings all home influences and teachings with him to school, whether they are good or bad. At school, the teacher tries to deliver an established curriculum, but it cannot be done successfully if void of the home influences the child brings with him to school. Therefore, in the success of the child, all three parties—home, school and child—must work in partnership. The school receives immediate benefit from the foundational behavior management established at home.

COMMUNICATION

On-going communication between home and school is most essential for the monitoring of both learning and behavior. Likewise, it is important that children recognize at all times that their parents and teachers are working together, so that they do not play one against the other. Wherever there is disagreement by either party, the issue should be discussed and settled between both parties in the absence of the child. To do otherwise will bring confusion in the mind of the child, possible disrespect for either party and lead to escalating problems in learning and behavior.

In my own experience as a parent, in addition to on-going verbal communication with school, I maintained that link through the innovation of a home-school notebook. I prepared a page for each week and asked the teacher to check behavior and work each day as good, fair or poor, followed by comments where necessary. At the end of each week, my child was rewarded based on his total ratings for the week. As he got older, the reward system took the form of points which was later converted into cash to meet specific needs or desires. As Richard, my son, indicated earlier, each term school report was also a source of accumulating points. Points were allotted according to grades received for each subject putting a total summary points on each report. For example, for each "A" grade, he would be allotted three points; for each "B" grade, he would be allotted two points; and for each "C" grade, he would be allotted one point.

At SFEC, we seek to bring parents into the habit of reinforcement for desired behavior, linking it to the point system used by the school. Parents are encouraged to award their children at home on a weekly basis based on their point standing at school for the week. This process works as an introduction to reward and consequences in a systematic way, leading to the parents' development of their own system at home, we hope.

One parent who attempted to apply this system reported on the effect. On two occasions, she deprived her child of technological equipment because of poor behavior and negative report from school. Her transformation in behavior was phenomenal. She switched from an outrageous, disruptive, boisterous and uncooperative student to a calm child with controlled behavior constantly seeking affirmation from her teacher and principal that her behavior was in order. Her cell phone could be used as a source of reward or consequence, which regulated her performance and behavior both at home and school.

EXPECTATIONS

It is well accepted that parents' expectations have a powerful effect on children's academic performance. Parental involvement in the school life of the child with special needs should not be viewed and defined in too narrow terms—such as direct involvement in homework completion—because the specific skills and patience required would prohibit many parents from being involved in that way. However, a strong form of parent involvement is expectations. Parents who hold reasonable expectations for their children with special needs can communicate these clearly and encourage their children to work hard in order to attain these both academically and in behavior. This can make a difference in a student's success.

Parents expectations of the school are also an important factor. If the child knows that his parents are satisfied with the performance of the school, the child's motivation for working hard will be greater, because he must now live up to the standard of the school or run the risk of exclusion. He cannot blame the school for his failure and neither can he fool his parents.

As revealed in the feedback from the research among parents in Chapter 8, parents comments point to the fact that while not totally dissatisfied, their expectations of the school were greater than what they were seeing.

I believe that some of these expectations are rooted in the parents' own difficulty in accepting the fact that their children have limitations and that they may not reach a level of achievement equal to non-disabled children despite their enrollment in a special school. While not negating the fact that there is always room for improvement in teacher competence, the outcome of the research pointed to the need for greater parental acceptance of their roles in the education process for their children..

VALUE ON EDUCATION

The value which the family places on education, es-pecially the education of the child with a disability, is also a contributing factor to the child's progress. If chil-dren are from a family which sees the child with a dis-ability—especially behaviorally challenged—as a nuis-ance to be tolerated rather than a child to be em-braced, then the family's involvement in his education will be less. When I called my first Parent Teachers' meeting after the inception of SFEC, I was shocked at the low turn-out of parents. I thought that based on the category of children we were serving, every parent would see the necessity to attend such a meeting. I was in for a rude awakening.

While not taking attendance at meetings as a full in-dication of the parents' value of education, it does give an indication of priorities. Parents are busy making a living for the family, and so must prioritize the use of their time. Failure to attend meetings to discuss the educational needs of their children with special needs and without an excuse could indicate that cooperation with school providing such education is not a priority.

As indicated in Chapter 8, parents' greatest appreciation of the school was the individual attention received by their children, followed by the encouragement, love and care that they and their children received. The small classes and the progress of their children went hand-in-hand, while the individualized program and the teaching/learning process were less recognized by parents, possibly because these aspects were not as readily observed by them. This result could indicate that although parents are interested in the progress of their children and expect the teachers to give the necessary care, they are less concerned about the process of getting these results. It could also be one of the reasons for their poor attendance at meetings.

GENERAL VALUE SYSTEM

In addition to the parents' value of education for their children with special needs, the general value system of the family also may impinge on the level of cooperation the school is likely to receive from parents. If emphasis may be placed on material things rather than education, then it will be likely that children's values will be misplaced. It is the belief of some teachers that the value of some of these children is reflected in them just wanting to carry the latest cellular telephones and being in the latest fashion rather than having the necessary books for school. Hence we see the emphasis on the tight pants being altered in keeping with the latest fashion rather than allowing for the following of the school rules as a necessary part of their education. Students will also be given the latest name brand bag and shoes but there are no books in the bag.

FAMILY SETTING / DYSFUNCTIONALITY

Where children are suffering from adverse circumstances at home, as is the case with a number of the children mentioned in this book, parents need to work even closer with the school in helping the children to deal with their situations while giving necessary attention to their education. This situation is the most difficult of all. Parents need to be honest with the school in explaining the child's situation, rather than attempting to cover up the unpleasant truths while depriving the child of possible help and support.

Schools need both guidance counsellors and social workers in full time or part time service. Parents must work collaboratively with the school in keeping appointments and doing follow-up work with each child. At SFEC, our most significant successes with behavior change have been with children whose parents are consistent in attending counselling sessions at the school, keeping appointments for outside intervention in child guidance clinics, and carrying out follow-up work with the student at home. Such was the case with Noel, who was vigorously rebelling against his adoptive status and resorted to disruptive and self-destructive behaviors. His adoptive mother, who was also subject to abuse from him, faithfully followed through the processes of repeated conferences with the school. In addition, she accepted referral for psychiatric assistance, and kept appointments at the clinic consistently even in the face of outrage and violent rebellion from Noel.

Change for him was incremental and often too insignificant to observe, but it was happening. While his attitude toward counselling was one of rebellion in the outset, he gradually became comfortable with the psychiatrist and even anticipated each visit. The significant change began when he was placed on part-time attendance. He made small steps in respect for school authority with a desire to please, first at the level of the principal and, at a much slower rate, to his form teacher. When in private, he was at times almost humble, and one could detect some change coming from the inside while at other times in the presence of his classmates, he tried to maintain his 'macho' image. Like Alrick mentioned in Chapter 8, Noel eventually came to himself and desired uninterrupted assistance from his teachers to prepare for his grade nine examination in order to move on to the secondary school of his choice. He was reinstituted full-time, and settled down enough to accomplish his goal. He sat the examination, got grades in the eighties and nineties, and at the time of this writing is attending the technical high school of his choice. His mother reports that he has settled down satisfactorily in this new school.

Both parents and school must join forces in the kind of support given to the child within accommodations necessary at both home and school. For example, if the school decides to ignore certain minor maladjusted behaviors while focusing more fully on others, it will only be effective if the family agrees to do the same. It is important that the child does not receive mixed signals between home and school.

Parent involvement has been shown to be an important positive force in a child's life. Therefore one must expect the two most important environments in child development—home and school—to increase their collaboration. With the increased difficulty of working with children with special needs, especially with a behavior component, the school calls for all the support it can get.

APPEAL

Parents, your special child is a gift from God. Cherish that gift. Yes, it is a great challenge working with your child, but the reward is as great. At the end of the day, you must be able to say, "I did my best in every aspect." No one can outdo this, and there is no failure. Your satisfaction will be evidenced in the peace that you experience. There is no greater job on earth than parenting, and what God asks you to do is to be faithful in your parenting role, and trust Him to do the rest. .

Love your child and take responsibility for his training (Proverbs 22:6). Take advantage of all of the help and support that is available to you. Play your part well in the school to which your child gains entrance. Be thankful for the opportunities opened to you. Let your complaints and expectations be reasonable, and be watchful of how you influence your child's behavior by your own values and attitude. Experience the joy of parenting your child with exceptionality.

Chapter 11:
The Place of Teachers

Teachers! Teachers! Where would we be without teachers? What educational programme could we have without them?

Teachers are vital in every educational programme, but the teacher required for special education is a different kind of professional. Of necessity, these teachers must have something more. They must 'have a heart' for this specialized area of teaching.

Working with children with learning disabilities and behavior disorders requires high levels of tolerance, understanding and patience. Results are slow in coming, and extrinsic rewards are often remote. What then can be a teacher's motivation for choosing this occupation? This question can best be answered by some of the teachers themselves, and in this chapter, I hope to reveal some of the answers in addition to highlighting the importance of the work of the teacher.

Perception

The teachers' function begins with a child facing him/her. He/She must first begin by seeking to know

the child and all he comes with. How the teacher perceives the child and how the child perceives himself
are major factors in the pupil-teacher relationship
which must be established. When students initially
enter the education system, the teacher cannot be sure
what that student's perception of self entails. For in-
stance, in the case of a child with a behavior disorder,
he may enter the school already feeling bad or incapable. The teacher who shares a similar perception of
him can only bring about this negative result.

Most of the students who enter SFEC come in with
negative perceptions of themselves. When they come
to us at age 12 or 13, they have already experienced a
string of failures in both academic performance and
behavior disorders. Many of them have felt the consequence of their behavior by being rejected at home
and excluded from schools. Their self-perceptions are
strongly negative.

The teacher's role is to restore a positive self-percep-
tion in the minds of these broken children. Teachers
therefore need to bear in mind what their roles are in
transforming these young minds and in fulfilling their
responsibilities to these students and society.

Teachers should educate themselves about the ex-
periential background of their students in order to better understand how they perceive themselves, and
what are their expectations, needs and aspirations. One
needs to bear in mind, that whenever a student enters
the school system, that socialization has already begun.
Therefore, the student comes with certain attitudes
and values already in place. Depending on his exposure
prior to the school experience, he might not see the

need to learn to read and write. One student at SFEC actually remarked that he did not need high grades for reading or writing, because his community leader earned much money and he could not read.

The teacher of children with special needs has the responsibility of addressing and transforming the children's perceptions of themselves while at the same time possibly modifying his/her own perceptions of the children. He/she must believe in the children and help them to believe in themselves, regardless of what they may have been led to believe previously about themselves. The teacher must be careful not to perceive all students in the same mold, because each child is different in more than one way. This is what makes each of them special.

FACING THE CHALLENGE

The teacher may be cognizant of all that is discussed above, some of which he/she would have learned during the job interview and orientation sessions. However, he/she soon learns that theory and practice do not always fit together nicely. When faced with more than one of these children with bad behaviors while trying to teach them academics, the real challenge surfaces. This was my personal experience as outlined in Chapter 1, and I can safely say that it has been the experience of all teachers working at SFEC. Working with children with behavior problems is a difficult job. This difficulty is magnified when dealing with more than one such child at the same time. So the question is "How do the teachers manage?"

As outlined in previous chapters, there is an estab-lished behavior management structure which is ap-plied; this is effective when each student in the class is thinking rationally and is in a cooperative spirit. How-ever, this is not always the case. Further, when one child comes to school in a bad mood, he has the po-tential to disturb the entire class. The teacher must manage the case carefully in order to prevent an explo-sion and maintain a harmonious learning environment.

In most cases, it is the conflict between students that creates the disturbance. Some of these begin after school on their way home but can filter back into the classroom, resulting in various degrees of name-calling and threats. A class or the entire school must engage in periodic conflict resolution exercises. We do this by applying the principle of restorative justice explained below.

All students and teachers in the class or the school sit in a circle and talk. One person is given the bulb marked 'restorative justice'; only this person can speak. If another person wants to respond or make another point, he/she indicates so by the showing of a hand. The leader of the session then passes the bulb to him/her. In the case of the class, the teacher is usually the leader; in the case of the school, the principal or her designate is the leader. That discussion continues usually for an extended period of time while the leader asks probing questions to unearth the source of the conflict and arrive at an agreement for resolution. Often the resolution requires apologies and commit-ment to refrain from a recurrence of the behavior. The students refer to this session as 'circle talk' and sometimes request it. One student would come up to me and say, "Auntie Claire, we need to have a circle talk." This often happens when a feud unseen by the teacher is brewing.

There has also been times when a teacher has had to deal with an outburst from a student—a frightening experience. For example, one of our students with Oppositional Defiant Behavior (ODD) became very angry, because the teacher confronted him about an offence which he had created. He denied the offence, and worked himself into an uncontrollable rage. He was about to hit the teacher and everything that came into his path. It took the effort of other strong students to restrain him, while another teacher spoke softly in his ear, giving him words of affirmation and encouragement and thereby gradually calming him. Of course, discipline was not left undone.

He received a time-out from school the next day, and the following day was required to come with his parent. By then, he was both penitent and frightened about the rage he had displayed. He acknowledged his own fear of the dangerous things that he was capable of doing when in such a state. He admitted that he was incapable of stopping himself once he had reached that level of anger. It is seen here that in the midst of his outrageous behavior, he was inwardly crying out for help.

In working with these troubled children, the teacher's attitude is what makes the difference. Where a teacher shows concern and patience with the child failing in behavior or performance, that child is encouraged and receives an opportunity to improve in an attempt to receive positive attention from the teacher.

Where he fails, he is corrected and offered help in a non-threatening way.

Even if the child has to be moved to a special education facility, such as SFEC, it should not be before other options have been explored. The child is then in a position to accept the new placement in a positive way and is more likely to continue to do his best without injury to self-concept.

Teachers who maintain a positive attitude towards children with special needs will not hesitate to make the necessary accommodations to facilitate both learning and behavior change. At SFEC, the teachers have to be alert to the need for such accommodations.

For example, Francine, who is on the Autistic Spectrum Disorder (ASD), uses very little verbal communication and her writing is illegible. She begins at the top left-hand corner of the page, proceeds diagonally across the page towards the bottom right hand corner, all in scribbles. She is very moody, so one never knows what to expect in her behavior from one day to the next. Her teacher teaches her at the individual level and positions Francine close to her at all times, breaks down her work into small segments and corrects each part of the work completed before proceeding to the next step. Only the correct answers are marked. Where there is error, the teacher gives the correction orally and allows Francine to make the correction before marking it. Since Francine is almost non-verbal, her teacher reads words, phrases, or sentences in oral tests and has Francine point to the content read. For expressive writing assignments, Francine is allowed to complete these on a computer.

Although there are specific rules for the classroom agreed upon by all the students, exceptions are necessary for some children regardless of complaints from other students.

Abigail has difficulty understanding the rules. She is easily confused, and her reasoning capacity is low. Her teacher acknowledges and praises her for each rule that she carries out successfully, although to the other six students in the class they do not see why she has to be specially mentioned or praised. Students with ADHD and ODD have been accommodated by allowing them short breaks between assignments, time out of seat to run errands, etc. and ignoring inappropriate behavior that is not drastically outside of classroom rules.

JOB SATISFACTION

Louise Strydom of the department of Psychology, University of the Free State, South Africa, argues in her article "Job Satisfaction Among Teachers of Special Needs School" that low job satisfaction in special education could be a reason why many teachers at special schools resign. She highlighted the need for teachers in these schools to cope with curriculum changes and the administrative duties that come with these changes, while dealing with these learners of diverse needs. These factors and others place heavy demands on teachers and can be extremely stressful. Therefore, the majority of teachers will not choose this field for a lifetime career. Some may work with special needs students for a few years but then move on. However, there are a few who find satisfaction in this service to children despite the challenges (Strydom, 2012).

In my many years of experience in special education, I have seen a few of these teachers who are comfortable in their jobs with special needs children, despite the stress. In the case of SFEC, our children come with emotional, social, neurological and behavioral problems in addition to learning difficulties. Therefore our teachers operate under great stress. Yet, throughout the life of the school, SFEC has retained its teachers with minimal changes.

In the research done among teachers of SFEC, when asked about job satisfaction and fulfilment, the summary of their responses was that they received fulfillment from students' progress in academic achievement, behavior, attitude, and respect of others. They valued the small size of the school which helped to facilitate a sense of family. This latter point also reinforces that small classes are an attraction for teachers in the special education profession.

While applying different behavior management strategies, and waiting for creeping results, the fact remains that the teachers are working in a hard place. They never know what challenge to expect with each passing day, and must gather the strength to cope under every situation. Yet to continue working in a hard place, and maintain a positive attitude, the job should bring some joy. In a mini survey, as part of my project for the course Overture 1 at the Bakke Graduate University, I asked the teachers to give me an answer to the question, "Would you say that Sure Foundation is a place of joy?" Here are some of the responses:

Joy is the emotion of great delight or happiness caused by something good or satisfying. Can a teacher working with disruptive behaviors which confront her every day be joyful? As a teacher at Sure Foundation Educational Centre, my answer is yes. I always remember that I have to play many roles, and I try to fulfill these roles with the help of God and my co-workers. Most importantly, I gain satisfaction from helping a child to develop self-management and the confidence necessary to overcome the challenges of his/her disability. Many times, my patience is tried, and I am tempted to give in and quit. Thanks be to God, the giver of joy, who reminds us in Psalm 126:5, "they that sow in tears shall reap in joy" and in James 1:2, "My brethren, count it all joy when ye fall into divers temptations." I therefore maintain and believe that rubies nor diamonds cannot give me the joy as when a student at Sure Foundation begins to build feelings of self-worth and experience success (JM).

The truth is, working at Sure Foundation Educational Centre has been a challenge with more down days than up days. At times, it even seems that one's best effort is a failure. But during that turmoil, as impossible as it seems, I find 'joy'. I find joy in knowing that as close as the age difference is between my students and I, and as much as they cross the line sometimes, they still find me as a confidant and a problem solver. I find joy in knowing that in some of their darkest and brightest hour, I play a part, even if it is a small one. My greatest joy, however, in working under these conditions is that while helping these children,

I'm helping myself because I've learnt to be tolerant, accepting, and patient. (SM)

The key word is joy. What is joy? For me, as a Christian, joy is not a fleeting feeling of happiness which results in a big, broad smile or bubbling laughter, although these could well be expressions of joy. Joy, however, for me, is an inner contentment that gives me the strength to do my best to bring out the best in others, and gratitude when I see some positive results in those with whom I interact. Therefore in spite of the stress, frustration, and even sadness sometimes, based on my perspective of joy, Sure Foundation is a place of joy. (JF)

The common thread running through these responses is that Sure Foundation is a hard place to work, but there is joy in the midst of the discomfort. For me, working in special education for forty-seven years, I ask myself the question, "What has made me do this?" No one has asked me to do it. No one has forced me to continue in it past standard retirement age. When I examine the state of my life, I realize that I have been experiencing joy in what I do. That is what has kept me—and the other teachers—working at SFEC. I get spiritual fulfilment from what I do despite the challenges. Seeing a child enter the school dejected, with low self-esteem, and a cast-away because of his behavior challenges, then see him walking out two or three years later with his head held high and a proud look of achievement moving onto his next phase of education is for me a source of joy.

TRAINING

Working in a special education institution/pro-gramme requires special training, which makes a difference in a teacher's ability to cope and achieve satisfaction in the process. Only teachers who achieve some level of satisfaction will stick to the task.

Training is essential before commencing the task as well as during the task. It is good that such a necessity is recognized and reinforced from the government level in Jamaica. Addressing the opening ceremony of the International Council on Education for Teaching's (ICET) 60th World Assembly on July 18, 2018, the Minister of Education, Senator Ruel Reid urged training institutions to ensure that more teachers are certified in special education. He said that they were trying to mainstream more inclusive education and require that teachers become more adept in differentiated instructional techniques.

While the minister emphasized inclusive education, it is the same training that is required for both inclusive and exclusive education. Students who must be pulled out of inclusive education because of the gravity of their situation must have teachers who are adequately trained for this change of venue and setting. Training must also be on-going, as new situations constantly present themselves. At SFEC, in-house training sits on the front burner. Training for teachers includes both practice and theory but heavily skewed towards practice. Our young teachers, who come to us as teachers' assistants, move on to college much more fortified to absorb the training received, as they have experience with which to apply new knowledge.

APPEAL

Teachers are key players in the business of special education for these children with the exceptionalities mentioned. Working with these children is a daily challenge. With training and an attitude of love, compassion, and belief in the children, teachers can experience joy, satisfaction and fulfilment. If you are a teacher already in this field, I encourage you to continue. Or you may be already attesting to what is written here. If you are a general classroom teacher or teacher in training, I encourage you to venture into this field. The satisfaction will always outweigh the difficulties and sacrifice involved. Our children need you.

Chapter 12:
Place of the Church

In Matthew 25, Jesus concludes his discourse with his disciples on the Mount of Olives concerning his second coming and the end of the world. Jesus gives three parables, which according to Matthew Henry, "are meant to quicken us all with the utmost care, and diligence to get ready for Christ's second coming." In the parable of the virgins (Matt. 25:1-3) and the parable of three servants (Matt. 25:14-30), Jesus reminds his listeners to be ready to present themselves to him and give account of their stewardship. In the third parable (Matt. 25:31-46), Jesus exhorts all people to be prepared to receive from him rewards or consequences according to how they spent their time on earth. In this Scripture, Jesus drew special reference to the treatment of the vulnerable and marginalized.

From these Scriptures, it is clear that God expects his church to be mindful of the needs of all persons, especially those falling into the category of the vulnerable and marginalized. Children with special needs fall in this category. Therefore the church cannot escape its responsibility towards these persons at the individual level or to ministries serving these persons. Those with disabilities are a part of God's creation, God's love, and God's plan for humanity.

MISSION OF THE CHURCH

Having answered Jesus' call, His people's first responsibility is to draw others unto him. In his ministry on earth, Jesus repeatedly told persons who received healing from him to go and tell others, so that they too would come unto him for healing of body and soul. Jesus' mission was to all people (Luke 4:18), and likewise, he sent his disciples to all people. "Go ye therefore, and teach all nations, baptizing them in the name of the Father, and of the Son, and of the Holy Ghost: Teaching them to observe all things whatsoever I have commanded you" (Matt. 28:19-20).

All people includes those on the fringes of society. It includes those in the ghettos of the city. If all people will be judged, then all people must be given the opportunity to hear and respond to the call. The marginalized might never come to church because of their positions of need, so the church must go to them. John M. Perkins, founder and president emeritus of the voice of Calvary ministries in Mississippi is a Christian minister, author, and community developer. According to him:

> Real change will come only when our leaders, filled with the Spirit of God and armed with a holistic gospel, relocate within the community of need. We must live among our people, agonize with them, make their needs our needs. Then we must join with them in solving their problems with God's power. (Perkins, 1982, 42)

The students of SFEC may never go to church, but they have needs for the gospel, and they need God's intervention to help them cope with their life situations. Therefore, the church cannot wait for them to come. The church must go to them in their school setting where it is easy to meet them. The school is a prime place for evangelism. When we consider students with behavioral disorders, it provides even more fertile ground. It is coming face to face with the real world.

The four Gospels—Matthew, Mark, Luke, and John—tell the story of Jesus and His mission on earth. Luke records this mission as spoken by Jesus Himself and foretold by Isaiah, the prophet (Isa. 61:1). It can be seen that his mission is weighted in favor of the vulnerable —the poor, the broken-hearted, the captives, the blind (disabled), the bruised (Luke 4:18). Then throughout His ministry, we see Him fulfilling this mission in His teachings and actions. Those who have answered the call of salvation must now exercise faithfulness to God for the sake of all people who must face judgment one day. This task is a matter of urgency, since no one knows the day or the hour when the Lord shall return with his angels to judge the world.

JESUS' CARE FOR THE VULNERABLE AND MARGINALIZED

The Bible's position on care and ministry to the vulnerable or those on the margins of society is very clear. References abound throughout the Bible drawing attention to the lost, the least and the last. Jesus said:

For I was an hungered, and ye gave me meat: I was thirsty, and ye gave me drink; I was a stranger, and ye took me in: Naked, and ye clothed me: I was sick, and ye visited me: I was in prison, and ye came unto me. Then shall the righteous answer him, saying, 'Lord, when saw we thee, a stranger, and took thee in? or naked, and clothed thee? Or when saw we thee sick, or in prison, and came unto thee?' And the king shall answer and say unto them, 'Verily I say unto you, Inasmuch as ye have done it unto one of the least of these my brethren, ye have done it unto me.' (Matt. 25:35-40)

Jesus mingled with sinners and further declared that He came not to call the righteous but sinners to repentance (Luke 5: 32). He demonstrated by His actions that in order to bring them to repentance, he needed to meet them where they were. He begins the Sermon on the Mount by pronouncing blessings on the poor in spirit (Matt. 5:3). In the text (Matt. 25:35-40), Jesus declared without a doubt the extent of God's seriousness about the treatment of the vulnerable.

Children with Learning Disability (LD) and Emotional Behavioral Disorder (EBD) are considered among the least of society. They are rejected by society and subject to much abuse and neglect. They are among the poor—spiritually, physically and socially—and so they are included among those to whom Jesus refers in the text.

Jesus showed compassion, love and care in his ministry on earth. He healed many persons who were sick and disabled, including the centurion's servant (Matt. 8:5-11), the woman with the issue of blood (Matt. 9:18-26), two blind men (Matt. 9:27-31), the demonized mute (Matt. 9:32-34), the man with epilepsy (Matt. 17:14-21), the man born blind (John 9:1-41), the crippled woman healed on the Sabbath (Luke 13:10-17), the ten lepers (Luke 17:12-19) and Blind Bartimaeus (Mark 10:46-52). If the church is to represent Jesus on earth, then it must copy Jesus in carrying out the great commission. Therefore, a person's poor behavior is no excuse to treat him badly. Most of the children who attend Sure Foundation Educational Centre (SFEC) are poor in their behavior, but Jesus expects people to treat them with kindness, love and understanding.

THE CHURCH IN THE SCHOOL

At SFEC, we have brought the church into the school. As mentioned in Chapter 6, daily devotions is a strong part of the school's programme. In these devotions, students are taught the love of God and invited to accept him and obey his Word. The staff shares fellowship with the students in all forms of devotion, and prayer meetings are held among the staff. The whole ethos of the school is one of Christian flavor. In fact, the logo for the school is an open bible with a torch, and that speaks for itself.

Rev. Exley Gayle, as the chairman of the school, leads the full school devotion once per month and interacts with the students. He sees this experience as extremely meaningful and fulfilling. In his own words:

I believe the church can and should be involved in the work of the school for adolescents with learning and behavior problems, especially the behavioral aspect, as the church is more equipped to help with the change in behavior through the Word of God. The Word of God has the ability to transform lives. Mark 4:26-29). I get spiritual fulfilment and personal atisfaction from the improvement in students' learning and behavior that I observe over time.

We also apply the Word in counselling students individually according to their individual needs. Mrs. Marie Tenn, who is the chief counsellor in this aspect, sees evangelism as an essential part of the school's mandate. In her words:

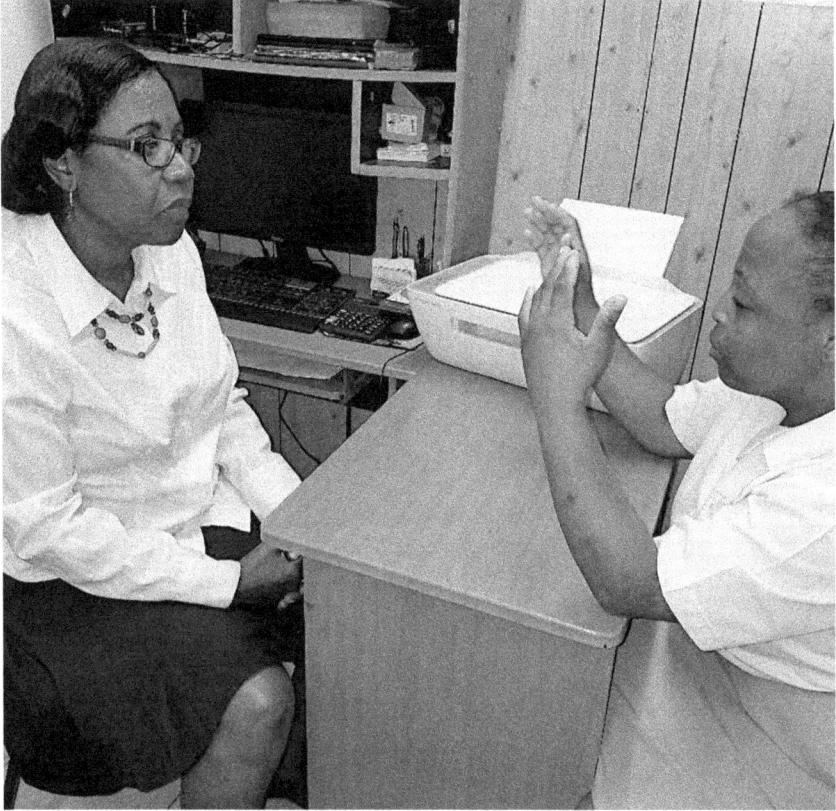

The attention of youths can be gained through love, intercessory prayer and selfless sacrifice of our time, talent, and treasure. This has been my experience at SFEC in counselling children who have come to me repeatedly with their problems. I do so by sharing with them about the love of Christ who is closer than a brother. Even when their parents fail them, we remind them of the scripture, that the Lord will take care of them (Psalm 27:10). God, through Christ, is interested in specialized evangelism for different groups (1 Cor. 9:22), and this includes persons with disabilities. I gain satisfaction from knowing that they feel free to come to me, thereby giving me the opportunity to minister to them.

In addition, the teachers' attitudes toward and treatment of the children is guided by Christian principles. For most of them, this is the only church that they know, because neither they nor their parents attend church or Sunday school. In keeping with John Perkins' recommendation, the church must go to them. So we take the church to them at school where we meet with them.

We can safely say that those of us working inside the school with these children are fulfilling God's expectation of us. However, that is not enough. God expects more from his church. I believe that the church has an important role to play in the care and support of children with special needs. Furthermore, it has the responsibility to set the pace for other groups and individuals to follow.

RESEARCH AMONG PASTORS

In Jamaica, some pastors organize themselves in small groups referred to as Fraternals to provide support to each other. In the geographical region of the school, there are two such groups. I met with each group, gave relevant information about the school and elicited their reactions to it. I then explored the possibility of a partnership with individual churches within these groups. After my presentation and discussion, I asked the pastors to complete a short questionnaire with the following questions:

1. Would you agree that if children with learning and behavioral problems are left behind, they

Suggestions by Pastors

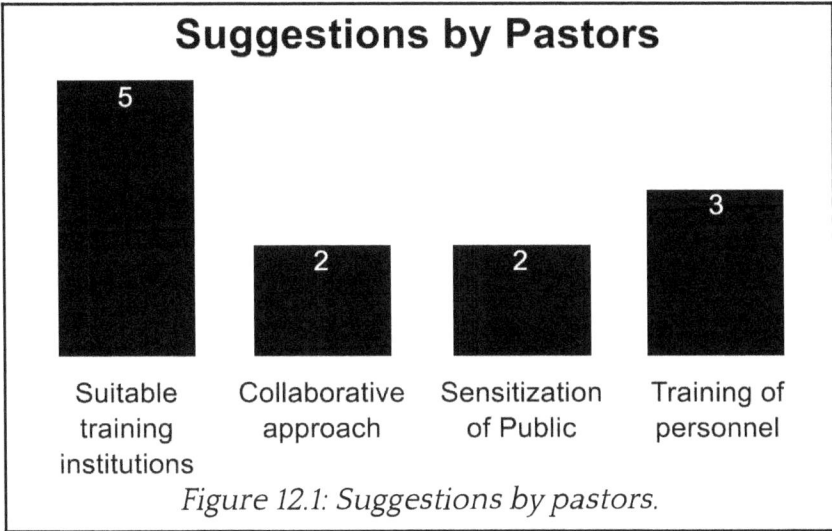

Suitable training institutions	Collaborative approach	Sensitization of Public	Training of personnel
5	2	2	3

Figure 12.1: Suggestions by pastors.

could be a threat to the social and economic fabric of the nation?

2. How do you think that the nation should address this problem?

3. What do you think is the role of the church in addressing this problem?

4. What do you think about the efforts of SFEC to address the needs of children with learning disabilities (LD) and emotional behavioral disorders (EBD)?

5. Do you think that your church will be willing to partner with our school in the following way?

   a) Your church provides support for the school by student sponsorship, or contribution to general operational cost.

   b) Our team include your church members in seminars on Stewardship, Theology of Work, and Christian Leadership at concessionary or no cost to you.

6. Would you be willing to promote the school through advocacy or recommendation?

The pastors present in both Fraternals attended to my presentation with interest, and some expressed their own ignorance of the work of the school in the community. After several questions for clarification, they completed the questionnaires in deep concentration.

In answer to the first question, eleven of the twelve pastors agreed that if children with learning and behavioral problems were left behind, they could be a threat to the social and economic fabric of the nation. One pastor was unsure about his thought on this matter.

Question number two was "How do you think the nation should address this problem?" The answers were coded under four headings illustrated in the figure 12.1.

The pastors gave priority to the establishment of appropriate training institutions to address the special needs of these children. Collaborative approach includes partnership between the private sector and the government. According to the pastors, a major part of the government's role was to train more teachers to handle the needs of these children.

The next question asked for their opinions of the church's role in addressing the problem. Most of the responses were meaningful:

- The church will have to mobilize all her resources to provide support
- Working along with such ministry in the redemptive plan of God

- The church should either provide trained persons or help to support institutions such as SFEC or partner with groups undertaking development of such children
- The church should provide mentorship, financial and spiritual support
- The church's position in the community will give it direct links to persons and help in identifying persons that need assistance.
- Address the existential and theological questions that arise from parents of such children. Channel funding to assist with their care.
- The church should be involved, ensuring that none is left behind. Can recommend and help to sponsor students.
- Helping and disseminating information and available resources to the general public
- Lobby government and other groups.
- Facilitate seminars and workshops.

These responses were encouraging. I realized that these pastors have an active interest in our work with these children and others equally marginalized; they were willing to share in the process of change, where necessary and possible.

The next question sought their opinions on the work of SFEC. Eleven of the twelve respondents commended the work of the institution with words such as "excellent, absolutely commendable; very good work; a wonderful ministry; being good stewards of God's grace; highly recommended." There was no response from

one person. These comments were similar to those received from business entities, which for me confirmed
that the work of the school is necessary and appreciated. This thought also lines up with the feedback from
parents, teachers and students.

Question number five asked for their opinions on the
willingness of their churches to enter into partnership
with the school as follows:

- The church provides support for the school
  by student sponsorship, or contribution to
  general operational costs.
- SFEC includes their church members in
  seminars on Stewardship, Theology of Work.
  and Christian Leadership at concessionary
  or no cost to them.

Eight pastors responded "Yes" to the proposal; two
persons answered "Not sure." One person stated that
he would first have to consult with the senior pastor,
and there was no response from the other person. The
final question asked about each pastor's willingness to
promote the school through advocacy or recommendation. All twelve pastors answered in the affirmative.

THE CHURCH OUTSIDE OF THE SCHOOL

From the responses above, the research revealed
that churches led by their pastors would be willing to
enter into partnership with the school to support its
programmes. Lack of knowledge about the school in

the community was also revealing. It means therefore that with proper promotion and information to the churches, greater involvement in the work with children—such as those at SFEC—could be harnessed through partnership. The answer to the question on the role of the church provided a fulsome response of how the church can serve the school on an on-going basis. In summary, they can do so by providing mentorship, financial and spiritual support, as well as entering into partnerships for the development of the children, while carrying out the redemptive plan of God and ensuring that no child is left behind.

APPEAL

Having answered God's call to lead a church, the leaders must realize that carrying out God's redemptive plan and purpose does not stop within the four walls of a church building. In fact, such limited settings could never contain the work of God among his people. Neither should the church be satisfied with serving just the people who enter its doors.

God's plan for humanity is inclusive of all people. His love extends to all people, and likewise his expectations from each person is without partiality, and his judgment is fair.

David Bosch (1929 -1992) was general secretary of the Southern African Missiological Society, and at the time of his death was professor of missiology at the University of South Africa. In his book, *Transforming Missions: Paradigm Shifts in Theology of Mission,* he rightly lists disabled persons among those considered as marginalized. Writing about the marginalized in the Jewish community, he had this to say:

> This applies to those who are marginal to the Jewish establishment. The Jesus story mentions them by names: the poor, the blind, the lepers, the hungry, those who weep, the sinners, the tax collectors, those possessed by demons, the persecuted, the captives, those who are weary, the heavy laden, the rabble who know nothing of the law, the little ones, the least, the last, the lost sheep of the house of Israel, even the prostitutes (Nolan 1976: 21-29). As happens in our own time, the affliction of many of those on the periphery of society is occasioned by repression, discrimination, violence, and exploitation. They are in the full sense of the word victims of society of the day(Bosch, 1991, 27).

Persons with disabilities are a part of God's creation, God's love and God's plan for humanity. If the church is to serve humanity as God expects, then it cannot turn a blind eye to work with the disabled wherever they are. Henry Blackaby, pastor of the Faith Baptist Church in Saskaroon, Saskatchewan, Canada, in his book *Experiencing God; knowing and Doing the Will of God*, implores us to observe where God is at work and join him there. Therefore, when the church sees people at work in service to persons with disabilities, based on the Scriptures, they should know that God is at work there and accept this as an invitation to join God.

Chapter 13:
Community Involvement

All of the students in the school are members of a community in the same way that they are members of a family. The adage "It takes a village to raise a child" holds true in every aspect of child rearing. In the community, all children belong to all members, because the whole community is affected in one way or another by the behavior and achievement of each child. Therefore, it behoves the community to be active participants in the development of each child through the formal place of learning, as well as community-based activities outside of the school. Adolescents with behavior problems should be of special interest and concern to all community members based on the negative impact that such behaviors can have on the peace and well-being of the community. The word 'community' here refers not only to the area in which the child lives but extends to include the community in which the school is located, as well as the wider community of the nation.

Whatever may be the dimension of the community, each is expected to play a role in the education of its children, because it is the primary beneficiary of the fruit of education. Persons with disabilities are equally capable of not just participating in society but contributing to it. Therefore the community should ensure that none of its children are left behind irrespective of their limitations. The community should work together with the school and other entities to promote the health, well-being and learning for all students.

BOARD OF GOVERNORS

School Boards are perhaps the most outstanding representation of the community at work in the school. Members of the Board give relentless, selfless, voluntary service for the governance of the school. At the same time, they are at the first point of accountability. In a non-governmental, non-profit school, such as SFEC, the commitment of the Board of necessity must go beyond service to include a financial contribution. Rob Martin, in a lecture on "The Donor Orbit and Motivation" at Bakke Graduate University, placed the Board at the centre of a gift supporting orbit which then spirals out eccentrically to include advisors, advocates, friends and acquaintances.

Further, Stanley Weinstein of the United States—musician and author of the book, *The Complete Guide to Fundraising Management*—points out that "One general rule in fundraising is that the Board of Directors donates approximately 15 percent of the contributed major gift income" (Weinstein, 2009, 35). At SFEC, all members of the Board are donors to the institution.

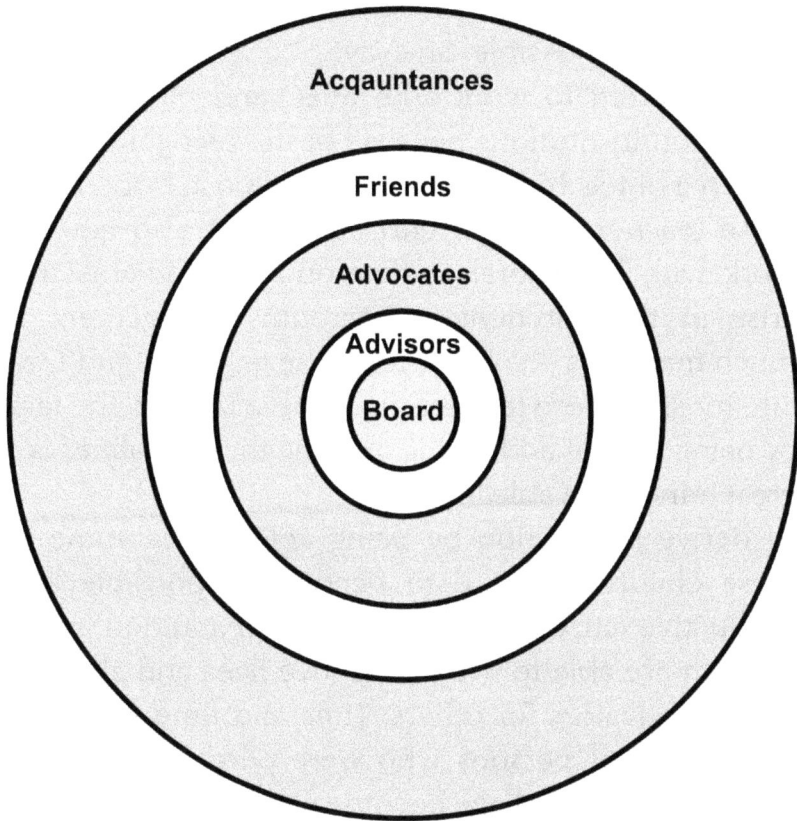

Figure 13.1 Donor Orbit

In addition to funding and governance, these members give voluntary service within the school itself as teacher assistants, devotional leaders, counsellors and accountants. They assume these responsibilities out of interest in the children with special needs and as a part of their contribution to God and the nation. Mrs. Adelle Brown, OD, retired Chief Education Officer in the Ministry of Education, is the vice chair of the Board and an encourager to the teachers who struggle in this area. She expresses her motivation to serve based on the recognition of the need for service and her confidence that success is possible. She says:

I am inspired to work with SFEC and other special education institutions because of the recognition that this area of teaching is tougher than most. Not only do these teachers teach a curriculum but also have to work with behavioral and emotional problems that arise in their students. Classroom management is much more of a challenge for these teachers, and I salute most of these teachers, who have risen to the task by being patient and caring. Honing these qualities is a great thing to be able to do.

I derive satisfaction by being able to see some of these children mature to become responsible and productive citizens of our country. In addition, some of them are able to live productive lives and also become motivators for others. Time and time again, we have heard of persons who were perceived to have special needs who have become world leaders and inventors. God bless this field of endeavor.

Other members of the Board concur with Mrs. Adelle Brown and express their satisfaction from serving on the Board. They said this because of the direction of the school in transforming the lives of these children, especially those with behavior problems. They saw wherein the school was leading them to be disciplined and respectful individuals with proper interpersonal skills despite their challenges.

Donor Relationships

The largest donor to the school, Mrs. Imogene Cooper-Rhoden, is also a member of the Board serving as secretary/treasurer of the institution. Her major donation takes the form of physical space to house the school in addition to sponsorship of individual students from the immediate school community of Grants Pen. In answer to the question of 'what motivates her to give so much for the school,' this was her response:

I work in a community of mostly low income and under-privileged persons, and I think that the school is providing a valuable service in lifting the educational standard, especially of those with disabilities. If one child is enabled, the community will be better off, and so as many as the school touches, the community is that much better off.

I get personal satisfaction from the knowledge that I am carrying out my God-given responsibility to help others, and the fact that so many students have passed through the school and doing well.

Business Entities

Ten business entities in the school community were interviewed about their possible support of STEC. Six of them offered to give support through cash donations for general operational costs and the provision of materials and equipment. They agreed to do so because, in their opinion, the school was providing a

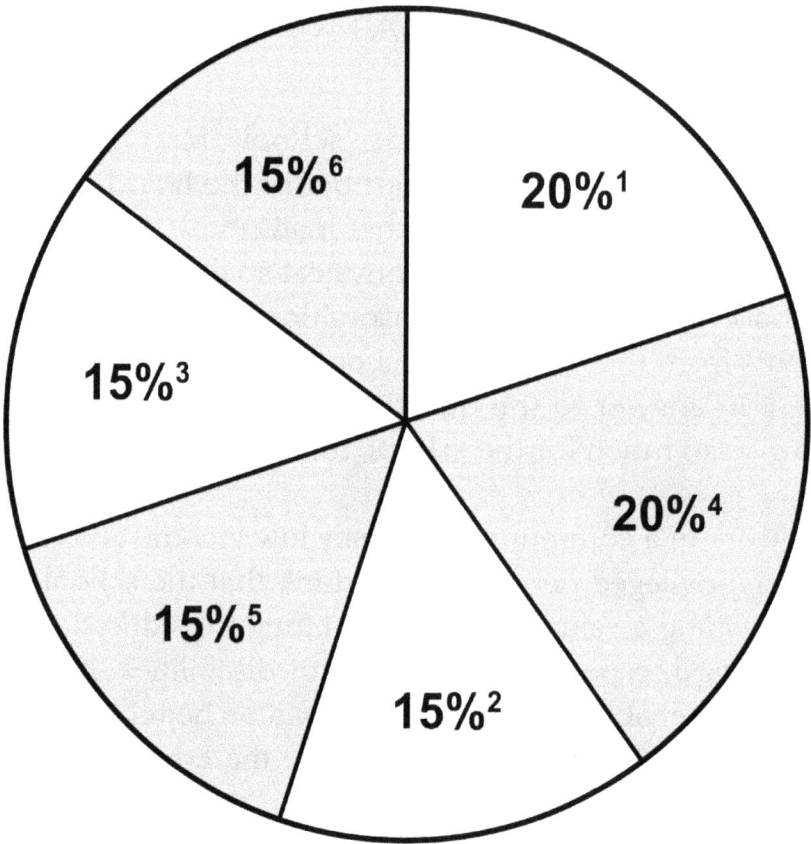

1. Early detection and Treatment
2. Appropriate programs by MOE
3. Training of educators
4. Small classes and one to one attention
5. Improved parenting skills & responsibility
6. Others

Figure 13.2: Suggestions by business entities

valuable service in a more effective way than the government would be able to do.

In response to a question, which asked for suggestions to address the needs of children with learning and behavior problems, respondents gave a number of suggestions which were coded and are illustrated in figure 13.2.

Early detection and intervention, small classes and one-to-one attention, appropriate programs by the Ministry of Education, improved parental skills and responsibility, and training of educators were all suggested by these business persons in the school community. It is clear that the operators of these businesses are knowledgeable about the true educational needs of these children, and so should be included as valuable partners.

It must be noted that all business entities referenced above are small businesses. The larger businesses were less available for interviews, and general support from those businesses have not been forthcoming. This could be as a result of the small size of SFEC, as well as its less influential capacity.

INDIVIDUAL DONORS

As noted earlier according to Rob Martin, every nonprofit organization has an orbit of supporters whom it can draw into donor relationships, starting with the Board of Directors at the centre and spiraling outwards to acquaintances. In my research, I targeted these people, and conducted personal interviews with them to enlist their support.

Fifty-one persons responded to the questionnaire inviting donor relationships, all of whom agreed that they were acquainted with SFEC, and that it deserved to be supported. In answer to the question of donations in cash and kind, a total of thirty-one persons agreed to be financial donors. The spread of the donors on the donor orbit is illustrated in figure 13.3.

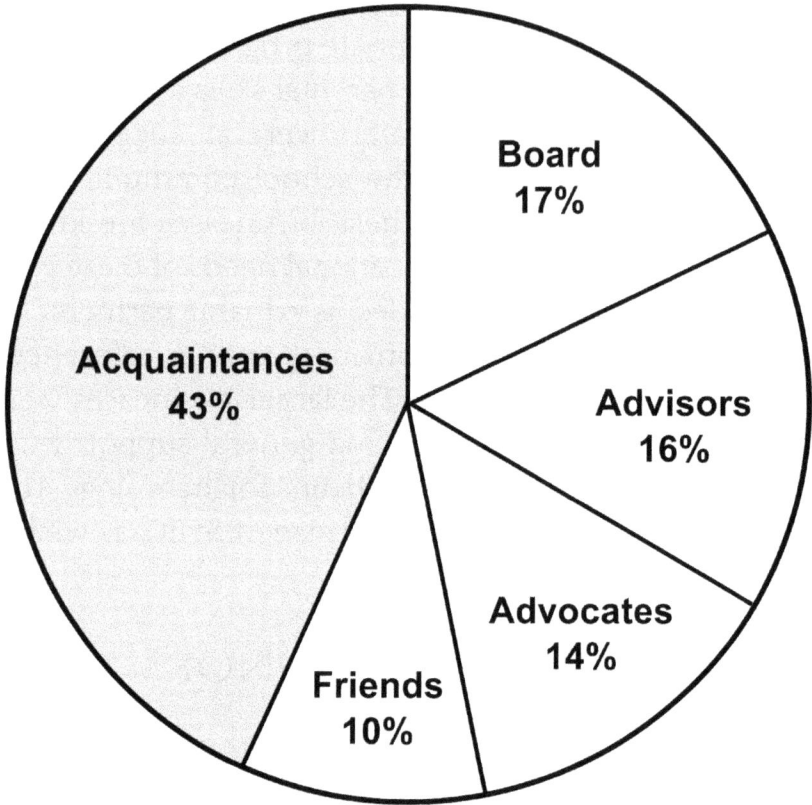

Figure 13.3: Distribution of individual donors on orbit

The Board, which is at the center of the orbit, is comprised of nine persons or 17 percent of the total number of donors. The next circle within the orbit is the advisors, which consist of eight persons or 16 percent of the donors. The advocates consisting of seven persons, or 14 percent of the donors, come next within the orbit. Then there are the friends comprising five persons, or 10 percent of the donors. Finally, in the outermost circle are the acquaintances, representing the largest proportion of the donors, that is, twenty-two persons or 43 percent of the donors.

Partnerships

Rob Martin, in his lecture, emphasized the importance of giving back to our donors, thereby establishing a two-way relationship. This may be done in the form of nurturing partnerships, so that each party receives some satisfaction from the exchange. Against this background, invitations have been extended to all donors to participate in special activities of the school that can bring them pleasure. In the case of businesses, the school has offered to reciprocate by offering training seminars in work ethics and other areas identified at no cost or at concessionary rates to their staff.

In this act of partnership, some companies offered skills training and work experience to our students. I consider the opportunity for students to attend work experience within walking distance of the school to be a great privilege. Further, I appreciate the positive responses from these companies that have potentials for long-term relationships.

Other valuable partnerships with the school community include services to the school by members of the community. These community members who are in employment to the school have a vested interest in the protection and preservation of the school, operating with a sense of community ownership. The inclusion of members from the community within our Human Employment and Resource Training (HEART) skills evening programmme also brings the community into the school and fosters community interest and support.

The school also benefits from volunteer service by members of the community in addition to that received from Board members. Voluntary services include skills training in the areas of visual arts, music and food preparation, all by members living in the community or attending church in the community. The school also brokered partnership with the library, whereby our students visited the Grants Pen Branch Library in groups at scheduled times. They received training in the use of the library and access to its use, with some activities specially designed to meet their needs.

In addition, the school has established partnership with the police station in the community for support in the behavior management of the students. They are invited to come in and give motivational talks to the students periodically, and they stand ready to respond to any emergency situation at the school. Thereby students learn to view the police in a positive and non-threatening light.

There is good collaboration with the community of Grants Pen in which the school resides. The school reaches out to the community, and the community reciprocates with goodwill towards the school.

However, it is the communities from which many of the children come and the varying degrees of dysfunctionality of their homes that is the greater challenge. They will try to conform to the rules at school, but when they get home, their homes within the community give a different signal, and they do not have the necessary coping skills.

APPEAL

My appeal to all communities is to look out for the child with exceptionalities and support that child and his family with love and understanding. A child with a disability or exceptionality can enter into our family at any time without warning by birth, accident or illness, over which we have no control. Let us be our brothers'—and sisters'—keeper in the community.

To the wider community of the school and the nation, let us be mindful that we have a God-given responsibility for the care and protection of these children. Let us give a helping hand towards their development wherever and in whatever way possible.

Be a good neighbor to a child with special needs. Avail yourself to be a mentor, formally or informally, especially to the boys. Be a watchdog for any special needs child in your community. Encourage them with their school work, and let them feel your love.

CHAPTER 14:
THE ROLE OF
GOVERNMENT

The involvement of the government in the education of children with special needs expresses itself in the form of legislation and provision for children with disabilities or exceptionalities. Provisions include instructional arrangements and procedures for evaluating and meeting the learning needs of these children. At a more practical level, it involves "individually planned and systematically monitored arrangement of physical settings, special equipment and materials, teaching procedures, and other interventions designed to help exceptional children achieve the greatest possible personal self-sufficiency and academic success" (Heward & Orlansky, 1988, 18). This description aptly fits what special education should involve, which, if effectively implemented, should satisfy the education of most children with special needs. It is incumbent on each country to establish legislation to ensure that these provisions are enforced to produce the required results.

LAWS AND POLICIES

I believe that the United States of America is one country which takes the lead in enacting laws and policies for persons with disabilities, thereby setting the tone for other countries to emulate. For example, there is The Education for All Handicapped Children Act, P.L. 94-142, which was enacted in 1975. The major features of the law are as follows:

1. a free appropriate public education must be provided for all handicapped children.
2. school systems must provide safeguards to protect the rights of handicapped children and their parents.
3. handicapped children must be educated with non-handicapped children to the maximum extent possible.
4. an individualized education program (IEP) must be developed and implemented for each handicapped child;
5. parents of handicapped children are to play an active role in the process used to make any educational decision about their handicapped children.

States meeting the requirements of P.L. 94-142 receive federal tax dollars to help offset the additional costs incurred in providing special education services (Heward & Orlansky 1988, 15).

In addition, there is the Individuals with Disabilities Education Act (IDEA), which require schools to provide free appropriate public education to all students within the regular education setting.

In my own country, Jamaica, at the time of writing, the policy on Special Education is in its final stage of processing and not yet enacted as law. The Special Education Unit of the Ministry of Education already embraces certain policies in its goals as stated below:

1. to promote equity and access to educational opportunities for children and youth with special needs at all levels of the education system
2. to promote a system of inclusive education where possible, recognizing that some children may be best served in segregated facilities or home/community based programs
3. to develop programs to promote maximum student success depending on the nature and severity of the exceptionality
4. to implement regulatory systems to govern the provision and delivery of special education services.

While one must applaud governments for attempts made to address the special needs of these children in the education system by enacting laws and/or developing policies, for these attempts to be more than theory, much work is required where it matters most, on the ground and in the classroom.

EQUITY AND ACCESS

Special Education is an expensive service and requires much more expenditure per capita for its effective delivery. For children without special needs, one teacher may adequately teach forty children, while it takes at least five teachers to teach that same number of students with special needs. It may cost the government five times more per capita in teacher salaries for children with special needs versus for other children. This cost does not include the additional expense for specialized equipment and facilities. The government also has the responsibility to make equal provision for the supervision of the education process. This factor has implications for finances, as more officers must be paid to supervise a smaller group of students.

Any government policy on equity in special education must be supported by a commitment to the extra expenditure necessary for the effective delivery of the educational program. Governments must be prepared to spend significantly more per capita for the education of children with disabilities/special needs. The main responsibility rests with those who have been entrusted with the expenditure of taxpayers' money. They must make decisions that benefit all citizens equitably. Persons with exceptionalities have equal rights to satisfy their educational needs.

INCLUSIVE EDUCATION

The policy refers to inclusive education where pos-sible. This approach has the effect of minimizing costs and hopefully improving the quality of education in an integrated setting. While this approach may be the perfect plan for children with mild to moderate disab-ilities, it is much less likely to satisfy the needs of chil-dren with severe to profound disabilities. The latter need an environment in which they can be free to be themselves and learn at their own pace rather than striving to match up with their schoolmates, which then becomes an additional stress factor for them and interfers with their rate of learning.

They benefit more from small classes and individual attention in a restrictive environment. SFEC is a re-strictive environment, but the positive factors associ-ated with its size outweigh that which they may have gained by being in an established, inclusive and less restrictive environment. This experience is endorsed by Bullock and Gable, who posit that for students with EBD, an environment that is highly structured may be considered the least restrictive environment for them (Bullock & Gable 2006, 13). Their point is, that in such an environment, a child may be able to thrive, learn new behaviors and make academic progress better than in a less structured setting.

Non-Governmental Organizations (NGOs) in Education

Most if not all the schools addressing the needs of children with severe to profound disabilities in our country were initiated by the church or private individuals, notable parents of children with special needs. The government often comes in at a later time, after the schools are established, granting support at various levels. This process relieves the government of the major cost of providing special education, since the schools operate largely by voluntary service and highly subsidized accommodation, as is the case with SFEC.

However, the government of the country has equal responsibility for the children in these schools, because they are the nation's children. For this reason, operators of these schools cannot have total autonomy but must operate in accordance with the established laws of the country relating to education.

SFEC is a private school started by an individual, the author of this book. It came as a response to an observed need for the education of children with LD and behavior disorders at the secondary level. However, the children who need the service has never had the money to pay fees which could cover the cost of their education. Therefore our school has existed on full or partial voluntary service and donation of facilities over its lifetime. Meanwhile, many private schools have had to close their doors because of financial incapacity.

FINANCIAL ASSISTANCE

While the government is not responsible for financing these schools, it has an obligation to render assistance for the benefit of the students to the same extent that it holds the schools accountable to operate under the jurisdiction of the education laws. SFEC has benefitted from government assistance in small grants and fees for students, without which the operation of the school and the number of children it serves would be greatly reduced.

Through the Special Education Unit, students who can benefit from our programme are referred to us, and contributions toward their tuition fee are paid by the government. At the time of writing, the government has undertaken to pay the full fees for students whom they refer. This is a welcome intervention, which should bring us closer to meeting the cost of operation. However, our fees still have to be kept at moderate rates that are affordable to private students who need the service but cannot afford to pay real costs.

SUPERVISION

Private schools also receive the benefit of supervision from the government. While demand is made on these private schools to adhere to the laws of operation, the government provides the necessary support seminars, workshops and in-house supervision. The Special Education Unit and Independent Schools Unit working in collaboration involve the school in all pos-

sible training opportunities, while the education officers—especially from the Special Education Unit—visit
the school periodically to provide support for administration and the teachers in the classroom.

APPEAL

While developed countries such as the United States
of America are making strides in policies for Special
Education, backed up by financial responsibility, developing countries such as Jamaica have much catching
up to do. The government of any country—even the
smallest and least developed—must give consideration
to the cost benefit of expenditure towards education in
general and special education in particular. In the case
of children with EBD, lack of adequate attention at
whatever cost could have far reaching negative effect
on both the social and economic fabric of any nation.

It is clear that the government of Jamaica is making a
growing input in the education of children with special
needs. This includes contribution towards private
schools carrying out such functions, as well as the establishment of appropriate systems in public schools.
However, a comprehensive long term plan to meet the
needs of all levels of children with exceptionalities is
desirable.

Despite the best efforts of the parents and the school,
there are some children with behavior disorders who
fail to respond adequately to intervention at these
levels, and so have the potential to become a threat to
the society. It is now incumbent on the government to
make provision for these children at the next level. The

school and family must appeal for support from this outer band of which the government is a major participant. Therefore, for children such as those attending Sure Foundation Educational Centre, the government needs to make provision to receive children whose behaviors fail to be positively affected by the efforts of the school and the parents.

These children must be placed in 'intensive care' to catch them upstream before they fall downstream. This care may involve frequent external treatment while remaining in their environment, or a pull-out from their home and school environment for specific periods of time in order to facilitate intensive and uninterrupted treatment. Of course, such intensive care may require substantial increase in expenditure for it to be effective, and so should form a part of the country's annual budget. This expenditure will be well worth it versus the cost of maintaining prisons.

CONCLUSION:
DOING WHAT THEY WANT
TO DO

I have shared my lifelong experience in the education of children with disabilities, both at home and at school. Although my greatest experience at school was with deaf and hard of hearing students, the emphasis here was on children with learning and behavior challenges. This is largely because my experience with these children started at home, and thereby gave me greater opportunity to relate to this kind of disability. It was my home experience that led to the establishment of the Sure Foundation Educational Centre, which now becomes my main point of reference. The experiences and testimonies outlined herein provide evidence that children with these disabilities can succeed despite their challenges.

Prior to coming to SFEC, many of them lacked confidence in themselves and hope for the future, because most comments made to them by parents and schools were about their negative behaviors. Children need to know and feel that despite their bad behaviors, "there is much good in them," as one teacher puts it. This approach is the way that Jesus would want persons to respond to them, that is, by treating them with grace (Matt. 19:14).

The evaluative research which took the form of an Appreciative Inquiry (AI) brought to light many positive things about the children in particular and the school in general. The purpose of the AI was to identify the positive core, which would lay the foundation for establishing a preferred future. The idea was to build on the good that already existed. The students' metaphorical images of the school in the future as a hospital represents a combination of their present experiences which they want to maintain and further refinement of that state. The capacity of the students to visualize the school in this way testifies to the fact that they are not of low intelligence. As adults, we must pay attention to this fact and treat them with the respect that they deserve by listening to their points of view.

The outcome of students attending the school has also provided evidence that children with behavior disorders can change and be transformed towards focused, productive and contributing adults in our society. The book posits that they can do this, given the appropriate climate and necessary support. The process requires a collaborative approach starting with the child's own desire supported by parents, teachers, community, church and government.

THE DESIRE FROM WITHIN

If there is one thing I have observed in my years of working with children and adults, it is that in the long run, people will always do only what they want to do. No amount of force will bring them into conviction of sustained conformity. They may do what they are told to do at specific times because of the rewards or consequences attached but not from the heart. And what does not come from the heart will not last. The employee does what he is told to do for the reward of his pay cheque. The student does what he is told to do for the reward of staying in school, even if his purpose is social rather than academic. Only what he does because he has an inward desire to do so will have the effect of changing his behavior or work attitude in a permanent way.

To effectively bring about transformation in the lives of children with learning and behavior challenges, one must begin by developing a desire in them that has the effect of leading to change. At SFEC, we have sought to find the mind of the child, and use that as the starting point to establish a programme of incentives that leads from one desire to the next. We seek to find out what truly interests the child, however small, and begin a reward system towards that desire.

It can be argued that the behavior was only for earning of the reward and not genuine, and therefore will not be sustained once the incentive is removed. This may be true, if the incentives are limited in time and quality. But as the incentives move from one level to another, the associated behaviors become ingrained into desires themselves. Several students have declared to me that they want to change, they are trying, but it is hard, and I believe them. They need the help of super-natural powers. That's why we pray for them consistently and lead them to the source for themselves. What is important is that they have a desire to change.

Those students who say they want to change are the ones who are likely to change. They will change in their attitude towards their work and behavior. The testimonies outlined in this book are from students who wanted a change in their level of achievement and in their behavior. Alrick began this process when, like the prodigal son, he came to himself, wanted a change and made the decision to put in the necessary effort. The results have been phenomenal and keep on growing.

Of course, they must be brought to conformity by whatever process necessary, but true transformation will only take place when that conformity is motivated from within. There are other students who conformed to the rules at school motivated by the incentives. However, after leaving school, they simply reverted to their former behavior.

If we are going to help children with special needs, especially those with behavior challenges, the best or only way to begin is to develop in them a desire to achieve change. This objective may take a long time to materialize, so patience is required. Yes, we must de-mand conformity but with the aim to take them to the next level—that of change from within towards true transformation of behavior and attitude. The role of teachers and parents must be to collaborate in their efforts to achieve this goal and work in tandem with all other available support.

A COLLABORATIVE EFFORT

Parents need to understand that they are their children's first teacher. Much of the child's progress in school and the world depends on the foundation that is laid at home. The teacher in the classroom cannot replace the teacher at home. Sometimes teachers also make the mistake of blaming parents for failing to do some things which may be difficult for parents such as helping their children with mathematics homework. Together, parents and teachers can be a powerful influence for the advancement of the children in their care. It is a strong harmony of home and school that is required to bring out the best in these children with learning and behavior challenges.

Every child who has come to SFEC and made exceptional positive changes in behavior and work attitude has had strong parental support. The work of the teachers has not been in vain, so some children have achieved even with weak parental support. However, the ones who excel are those with strong parental support. It must be noted that this support is not necessarily financial, though this may also be a part of the solution. Many of these supportive parents are from the most humble background, but they make themselves available in the best way that they can, have goals for their children, follow up their childrens' progress, cooperate with the teachers and work in harmony with the school. Parents of children with special needs should be led to understand that their role in the education process is critical and should be no less than their role in the education of their children without disabilities.

It is also the responsibility of the school to provide the kind of learning environment that is best suited for the specific needs of the children it serves. Children with learning and behavior challenges need a learning environment of love, encouragement and warmth as a baseline. The positive core of SFEC, as identified by parents, teachers and students include all of these factors. Other factors identified were the small classes with individual attention, family-type relationship and an award system to support discipline and improved performance. I believe that these factors must take priority in every educational facility for children with special needs. I recognize that additional tolerance is also necessary when dealing with children with behavior challenges, such as those arising from ADHD and Conduct Disorder.

There must be involvement from the community, which is the child's first place of contact outside the home. It influences the child directly and indirectly. The community is also affected by the presence of the child, because he is a part of it. The community cannot take a hands-off attitude towards the child with a disability, particularly if that disability involves behavior issues.

It is incumbent on the community to receive the child with LD and EBD as well as children with other special needs. The maxim, "It takes a village to raise a child" is especially relevant to a child with special needs. The community must watch over the children and give support to the parents through citizens association meetings and other support groups. Further, the businesses within the community must be open to receiving them at the appropriate age for work experience and employment, thereby helping them to gain independence and take their places in society as much as is possible.

The United Nations Convention for the Rights of the Child (Article 18) places a responsibility on governments to provide support services to parents, especially if both parents work outside the home. Article 24 states that equal education provision must be made for children who are disabled as well as those who are non-disabled. The government of a country is not asked to give patronizing favours to persons with special needs. While private schools such as SFEC will undertake to pick up the tab for children who are left drifting in the education system, government has a duty to embrace these institutions and give maximum help and support for the benefit of the nation's children.

The church cannot stand aside in all of this. It has a spiritual responsibility towards these children who are vulnerable and on the periphery of society. At the Pool of Bethsaida, there was a multitude of impotent people waiting for the water to be troubled by the angel who came once per year. The story is told of one man who could not get in, because his case was more severe than the others who came. He needed help to get in, but each year in the absence of such help, he missed the opportunity for healing while others more agile than himself succeeded, until Jesus came and rescued him (John 5:1-9). Like this man at the pool, Jesus will provide a way of escape for these children, and He is calling on His church to make itself available to be used by Him to bring about the necessary change in the lives of these children.

YES THEY CAN

With the collaborative efforts of child, home and school in an inner triangular effort, supported by an outer triangle of community, government and church, every child regardless of cognitive, social and/or emotional disorders or challenges can be transformed from within to accomplish their God-given purpose. May each of us who enter into the path of any of these children respond appropriately as the Lord requires of us.

About the Author

Clara M. Ricketts was born of Jamaican parents in Cave Westmoreland. She received her tertiary education from the Shortwood Teachers' College, the University of the West Indies, the Jamaica Theological Seminary, and Bakke Graduate University. She developed a passion for the education of persons with special needs from early in her career starting with the teaching of deaf children and then founded the Sure Foundation Educational Centre for children with learning disabilities and behavior disorders. She is a deacon at the Mamby Park Baptist Church, where she leads in the areas of discipleship and deaf ministry.

REFERENCES

Al-Yagon, Michal. (Winter 2005) "Socioemotional and Behavioral Adjustment Among School-Age Children With Learning Disabilities: The Moderating Role of Maternal and Personal Resources." *The Journal of Special Education* 40(1), 205 -217.

Blackaby, Henry, Blackaby, R., & King, C. (2007). *Experiencing God—Knowing and Doing the Will of God.* Nashville, TN: Life Way Press

Bosch, David (1991). *Transforming Mission: Paradigm Shifts in Theology of Mission.* Maryknoll, New York: Orbis Books.

Bower, Eli (1988) "Early identification of emotionally handicapped children in school," in *Exceptional Children: An Introductory Survey of Special Education,* 3rd. ed. William L. Heward and Michael D. Orlansky (Columbus, OH: Merrill Publishing Co., 170

Bullock, Lyndal M. and Robert A. Gable (2006) " Programs for Children and Adolescents with Emotional and Behavioral Disorders in the United States: A Historical Overview, Current Perspectives, and Future Directions" *Preventing School Failure,* 50 (2), 7–13.

Carson, Cari (june 2015). "Rethinking Special Education's 'Least Restrictive Environment' Requirement." *Michigan Law Review* 113(8), 1397–1426.

Cooperrider, David L., and Whitney, D. (2005). *Appreciative Inquiry: A Positive Evolution in Change.* San Francisco: Berrett-Koehler, Kindle Electronic Edition.

Cooperrider, David L. Whitney, Diana, & Stavros, Jacqueline M. (2008). *Appreciative Inquiry Handbook: The First in a Series of A.I. Workbooks for Leaders of Change,* Second Edition (San Francisco: Berrett-Koehler Pub.,Loc. 696.

Durand, V.M. (1990). Severe Behaviour Problems: A Functional Communication Training Approach, Guilford Press, New York., 11–14.

Geddes -Hall, Jennifer (2015). "The School Counselor and Special Education: Aligning Training With Practice." *The Professional Counselor* 5 (2), 217–224.

Hammond, Sue Annis. (1998). *The Thin Book of Appreciative Inquiry.* Plano, TX: Thin Book Publishing Co, Kindle Electronic Edition.

Heward, William L. & Orlansky M. D.(1988). *Exceptional Children,* Columbus, Ohio: Merrill Publishing Company.

Hyman-Anglin, Rhona (2006), *Education and Society: an Introduction,* Ian Randall Publishers, Kingston.

Jamaica Ministry of Education (2010–2013). A Comprehensive 3-year Strategic Plan for Special Education.

Jensen, Eric (2010) *Different Brains, Different Learners: How to Reach the Hard to Reach,* Corwin [Kindle Version]. Retrieved from http://www.amazon.com.

Manning, Gareth (April 2016) "Grants Pen residents say policing model failed." Retrieved from http://old.jamaica.gleaner.com/gleaner/20080518/lead/lead6-.html.

Minahan, Jessica & Rappaport, Nancy (2012). *The Behaviour Code: A Practical Guide to Understanding and Managing the Most Challenging Students*, Howard University Press, Cambridge, Massachussetts.

Niesyn, Mary E (Summer 2009) "Strategies for Success Evidenced-Based Instructional Practices for Students with Emotional and Behavioral Disorders," *Preventing School Failures* 53 (4), 227-233.

Obaid, Majada Al Sayyed (First Quarter 2013). "The Impact of Using Multisensory Approach For Teaching Students with Learning Disabilities," *Journal of International Education Research*, 75.

Perkins, John M.(1982). *With Justice for All*, Ventura, CA: Regal Books.

Ricketts, Clara M, Williams, N., & Worges, A. (2012), Social influences, cultural norms, environmental influences and biological factors negatively impact the development of literacy among boys in a private special education school in the Kingston metropolitan region, Department of Behavioural and Social Sciences, Jamaica Theological Seminary, Kingston, Jamaica.

Ricketts, Clara M. (2016). A Vision and Plan for the Growth of Sure Foundation Educational Centre: A model for Special Education as a means for the National Transformation of Jamaica. Bakke Graduate University, Dallas, Texas.

Stephan, *Jessica* (June 2012). *Teachers as Advocates in Special Education*, https://www.impatientoptimists-.org/Posts/2012/06/Teaching-and-Learning-Advocacy-for-our-Students#.WayBTciGPIU.

Smith, Sally L. (May/June, 2002. "Parenting Children with Learning Disabilities, ADHD, and Related Disorders," *Pediatric Nursing 28 (3)*. Reprinted with permission by Learning Disabilities Association of America.

Strydom, Louise (Jan. 2012). Job satisfaction amongst teachers at special needs schools, *S. Afr. j. educ.* vol.32 (3). Retrieved from https://www.research-gate.net/publication/262558088_Job_satisfaction_a mongst_teachers_at_special_needs_schools.

The Project Approach, (Feb. 2015) "What is the Project Approach?" Retrieved from http://project ap-proach.org/about/project-approach.

Weinstein, Stanley (2009). *The Complete Guide to Fundraising Management.* John Wiley & Sons, Inc. Hoboken, New Jersey.

Appendix A:
Students' Daily Record

Name of student: _____
Grade: _____
Key: LT—Loses Temper; DA—Defies Adults;
   AO—Annoys Others; V—Vindictive Behavior;
   SO—Swearing & Obscene language

[See table example on next page.]

Date	Completes work		Follows the rules (3)	Good Relationship (4)	Total	Comments					
	HW (1)	Class (2)				LT	DA	AO	VB	SO	Other

Appendix B:
AI Interview Guide

Sure Foundation Educational Centre Appreciative Inquiry—Bringing Out the Best in our Children

Introduction

Thank you for participating in this interview. We will be inquiring to learn more about our children, and how to bring out the best in them here at SFEC. Parents, teachers and the students themselves will be interviewed directly to collect best case stories on which to build the future. We will be talking with parents, teachers and the children themselves. The point is to move forward in achieving the vision to make SFEC be the best place for children with Learning Disabilities (LD) and Emotional Behavior Disorders (EBD) to maximize their potentials. Your input will be an important contribution to generate meaningful ideas and actions.

Many times in interviews, we ask questions about how things don't work well. This time, we are going to approach things from a different angle. We are going to find out about your experiences of success here so we can build on those experiences.

We will seek to interview as many teachers, parents and students as possible who have interfaced with our school since its inception in 2005. When the interviews are complete, everyone's input will be put together to identify qualities in our children and practices here at SFEC that make us unique. With those qualities and practices as a foundation, we will create specific future steps to build on our strengths. We will explore how our positive past, the best of our experiences, can help us become more daring and innovative as we think about our true potential as a special school.

During our interview, we will be exploring the following areas:

- Best Experiences
- Core Values
- The Privilege of Teaching/Parenting
- Supporting Conditions
- Wishes for the Future

We will be asking you questions in relation to these areas, and recording your stories. Let's begin.

BEST EXPERIENCES

What experiences at Sure Foundation Educational Centre (SFEC) has made you feel most fulfilled? Describe a time when you felt most engaged, motivated, and excited about your involvement here?

Tell me about your best teaching experience, a time when you felt most alive and engaged. What made it so rewarding? Who was involved? How did students' learn? How did students behave?

Describe the child/children you teach/parent in a positive way. Think of a time in when you saw them at their best. What did it look like? Tell me about it.

CORE VALUES

Tell me about the things you value most deeply, things about yourself, your relationships, and your work. What are you like when at your best?

What are the most valuable ways you have contributed to SFEC—your personality, your perspectives, your skills, your activities?

What are the unique attributes of this school that make it valuable to you as parent/ teacher?

THE PRIVILEGE OF TEACHING/PARENTING

Our function as teachers/care-givers of children with special needs is one of caring. Our children need love and understanding. As parents and teachers, the privilege to participate in the nurturing relationship with our children as God's precious creation, is what creates and maintains the passion for our work. We would like to acknowledge that passion and explore with you how to acknowledge and develop this in all of those who nurture children here at SFEC.

What were your hopes & aspirations when you chose to be (or found yourself) involved with the nurturing of children (a child) with special needs?

What is it about these children (this child) <u>today</u> that keeps you involved?

The privilege of caring for children with special needs has sparked in many of us the passion for caring for the vulnerable. Describe a situation in which you felt this passion.

Supporting Conditions

Tell me about the core, life-giving factors in your experience. What are the key ingredients, both internal and external that enable you to be at your best and have fun?

Wishes for the Future

What are three things we do best at SFEC that we should keep, things that should be amplified or preserved even as we change in the future?

Imagine that five years have passed, and SFEC is fully developed to educate children with Learning Disabilities (LD) and Emotional Behavioral Disorder (EBD). Describe what it looks like.

What three wishes do you have to make SFEC the best place to educate children with special needs especially those with LD and EBD?

APPENDIX C:
SFEC AI PROVOCATIVE
STATEMENTS

The statements below give a reflection of the type of school envisioned by all stakeholders. Here affirmation is given to many of the things we are currently doing, but expectations for development are also set forward. Therefore, the framework is set for the next phase of the research—the Design phase. Cooperrider et al points out that, "The Design is a provocative and inspiring statement of intension that is grounded in the realities of what has worked in the past combined with what new ideas are envisioned for the future." It is with this new understanding that we will now begin the planning process as a staff.

I have merged the provocative statements produced in both Dream sessions, and outlined them below:

We are a school that helps all children regardless of their learning difficulties.
We are a school that meets the needs of all our children regardless of the challenges and disorders diagnosed in them.

We are a school where parents, teachers, and children agree about the welfare of students and what they should learn.

Our school is providing individual attention to students regardless of the size of the school and the challenges faced.

Our school is one that maintains small class sizes in order to facilitate individual attention.

We are a school that gives individual attention to our special needs children preparing them for the world. We preach, we teach, we love, we care.

We are a school that willingly receives slow learners at whatever level they are at and take them to the highest level possible for them.

We are a school that loves, nurtures, and respects our children regardless of their circumstances

We are a school that maintains equality for all children with discrimination against none.

We are a school that recognizes the special needs of boys.

We are a school that is committed to bringing out the best in our children.

Our school is one of the most outstanding special schools in the island of Jamaica, and is well known as an excellent place.

Our school is one that is continually improving its resources.

We are a school that attracts financial support.

Our school is affordable to low income families.

Our school is fully sponsored making us financially independent.

We are a school that provides quality and subsidized lunches affordable to all students.

We are a school that is built on the Rock of Jesus Christ, and as written in Scripture will endure the storms of life. Our school maintains Christian principles.

Our school is firmly planted in the Christian faith and positive guiding principles.

We are a school that maintains Christian beliefs and instil them in our everyday activities, thereby passing on Christian values to young minds.

We are a school that believes in prayer and the Lord's guidance and protection.

Our school is a school fully equipped with computers, technological equipment and other resources for children with special needs.

We are a school that uses technology to equip and prepare students for the world of work,

We are a school that have all necessary facilities for special education.

We are a school that provide programmes which are specific to the needs of our children.

Our school has a variety of vocational skills, and sees skill training as an important part of education in preparing students for the world of work.

Our school is preparing students to their highest level to move on to further learning.

Our school has diverse extra-curricular activities to foster the rounded growth and development of our students.

We are a school which equips students to move on to mainstreaming as far as they are able and soon as they demonstrate readiness.

We are a school that uses multifaceted approaches for teaching and learning.

Our school is a place where academic progress is evident.

We are a school that has highly trained energetic special education practitioners.

We are a school that has caring teachers that understand the students and help them to learn new things.

We are a school that is adequately staffed to meet the varying needs of our students.

We are a school where teachers experience a sense of achievement.

Our school is a place with students who are positive and well behaved.

We are a school where there is on-going positive behavior changes.

Our school is one that has loving and caring students who willingly share with each other.

We are a school where children are motivated to do their best.

We are a school that prepares students to be winners and useful citizens in the future.

We are a school with a strong and supportive parent body, who works in collaboration with the school for all issues pertaining to the welfare of their children.

Our school has a child friendly environment.

Our school motivates students with tangible rewards.

We are a school that is strong in discipline.

We are a school that is actively developing group dynamics and leadership qualities in our students.

Our school is a haven that allows students to learn at their own pace.

We are a school that stands out in our community as leaders and achievers.

Our school operates as a family with love, care, and respect for each other.

We are a school that promotes good health and relationships with one another.

We are a school that provides a safe and secure environment for all persons in it.

We are a school located in an environment that is very accommodating.

We are a school with adequate play area to support the physical and social development of our students.

We are a school that is peaceful, relaxing, clean, well-furnished and quiet.

We are a school that integrates special needs students with other students to the social and academic benefit of both groups.

We are a school that has visionary, but realistic plans for the future.